Wiccan
Celebrations

Inspiration for Living
by
Nature's Cycle

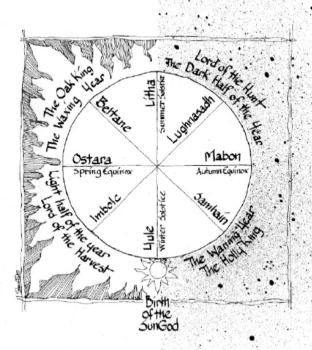

First published by O-Books, 2011
O Books is an imprint of John Hunt Publishing Ltd., The Bothy, Deershot Lodge, Park Lane, Ropley,
Hants, SO24 0BE, UK
office1@o-books.net
www.o-books.com

For distributor details and how to order please visit the 'Ordering' section on our website.

Text copyright: Silver Elder 2010

ISBN: 978 1 84694 538 0

A CIP catalogue record for this book is available from the British Library.

Design: Silver Elder

Printed in the UK by CPI Antony Rowe
Printed in the USA by Offset Paperback Mfrs, Inc

We operate a distinctive and ethical publishing philosophy in all
areas of its business, from its global network of authors to
production and worldwide distribution.

Wiccan
Celebrations

Inspiration for Living
by
Nature's Cycle

BOOKS

To Scott
For Inspiration all the Way

To my Parents, Ernst and Brigitte
for their Love and Insight

To all who celebrate Life and Love
by Nature's Cycles

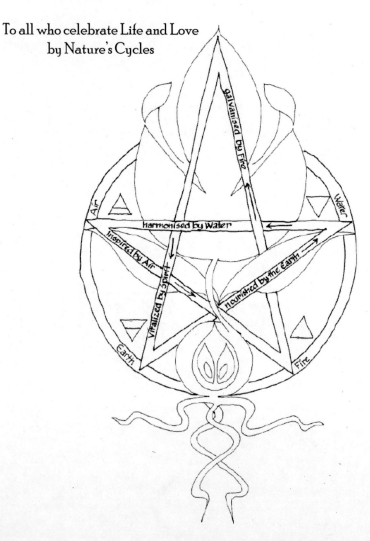

Special Thanks to Trevor, John and Stuart together
with the Team at O-Books for making
"Wiccan Celebrations" possible!.

CONTENTS

THE RITUALS

Preparation
Opening the Rite
Casting the Circle
Calling on the Quarters and inviting the Deities
Cakes and Wine
Banishing the Circle
The Closing Rite

The Esbat Meditations ~ Pg 213

Preparation
Opening the Rite
Casting the Circle
Calling on the Quarters and inviting the Deities
Cakes and Wine
Banishing the Circle
The Closing Rite

Esbats ~ First Quarter: Waxing Moon ~ Pg 236

Light

Esbats ~ Second Quarter: Full Moon ~ Pg 251

Time

Esbats ~ Third Quarter: Waning Moon ~ Pg 267

Many Chambered House

Esbats ~ Fourth Quarter: Dark Moon ~ Pg 280

Manifestation

The Charge of the Goddess

"As Above –
So Below "

Blesséd Be!

DEAR READERS

The Laws of Nature affect us on a daily basis in many ways, whether we are aware of them or not.

Our very lives depend on them as they encompass the Earth and the Elements supporting all of Life.

Nature's cycle manifests itself in our daily life and bio-rhythms as well as every stage of our life.

In Wicca, our quest is to live in harmony with Nature and the Divine in order to achieve personal integration to better understand ourselves, to help others and to understand our environment.

We do this by relating to the Divine and Nature's energies of which we are an integral part:
We are made by Nature to live by Nature's Laws to return to Nature once more at the end of our material earthly life span.

Our Planet Earth, as we are too, is part of the greater Whole; the Cosmos, and is therefore subject to the Universal powers and forces known as The All.

The Wiccan way seeks to understand, celebrate and live by these phenomena. I personally celebrate them, amongst other ways, through the written word which is a very powerful tool to express how much I enjoy and love what I sincerely believe in and do.

Hopefully it will also bring you as much joy and happiness!.

In Love, to Life!
May you blessed be!

Imbolc 2010

INTRODUCTION

Wicca is a Pagan magical mystery religion which encourages personal integration through living in tune with the Divine and Nature's Cycle, by celebrating her seasons, Moon phases, Sun rises, Sun sets, Moon rises, Moon sets, her sounds, smells, feel and rhythms.

Living in harmony with Nature is living in tune with her Energies, leading to greater sensitivity and creating a heightened awareness and perception.

Living in balance with Nature also leads to a greater openness to ongoing, ever developing and evolving spiritual growth, connection and integration.

Living in tune with Nature teaches us that All is alive and that the life force is manifest in All. All is therefore sacred and bears the blueprint of the Divine Source manifest as a binary force of male and female which we call the God and Goddess, complementing one another to form the Whole, The All.

We are an integral part of the All, having been created by the Divine Source of All, and therefore bear the blueprint of the Divine Source, giving us potential for a direct connection with the All, and the Divine, which are One.

The concept of Deity and the sacred in Paganism and therefore, also in Wicca, is not transcendent, but immanent and indwelling in all. The divine is therefore integral with ourselves; we are inherently divine. We respect Nature as all is alive and divine for we are a part of that All.

This makes Wicca the truly beautiful, wholesome, fulfilling, heartwarming, sincere and enriching experience offering a way of life that allows the individual to develop a genuine personal identity.

The content of this book is my personal celebration of the Sabbats and Esbats and is intended for Solitary or Coven use.

Hopefully it enriches and enlivens your life, as it did mine writing it.

Enjoy and Blessed be!

MORALITY

Good and Evil

The concept of good and evil is a definite part of Wiccan belief although they are not defined in the Judeo-Christian sense in the role of Christ, God and Heaven versus Satan and Hell.

There is no evil as Nature is our Spiritual Teacher with the Sacred and Divine residing within Her Ways. It resides within us all for we hold the Divine Spark being an emanation and manifestation of the Creation of Nature and the Divine Source of All Things, The All.

Evil, in Wicca, is perceived and understood as energies and powers counteracting the positive, the Light of Spirit and the Laws of Nature. It is the destructive force; the imbalance that will undermine the Will of Spirit and steer us away from the Light; the Divine and the Sacred.

Evil comes about as a result of man being divorced and separated from Nature and the Divine. Man is alienated from Nature by his disconnectedness and his lack of attunement to her in that he has lost his ability to hear his own inner voice through which Nature communicates; the voice of his inner Divine and the Sound of his Soul and Spirit.

Wicca as a religion and way of life seeks to reunite and integrate Man with his Divine inner Self through the Laws of Nature and Her Ways.

Wicca is a non-dogmatic belief system through which we create an awareness of the Laws of Nature to bring about an equilibrium between the Sacred, the Spiritual and outwardly rational. It seeks to create a living and working awareness of nature, its influence on

4

our daily lives and its energies thereby bringing about a balance in all aspects of life. Through this awareness, the Wiccan way hopes to unlock the latent potential for greater perception, heightened sensitivity and a general attunement to all energies within us and around us. This sensitization leads to greater integration within ourselves, our greater universal context and the Divine leading to a greater self-awareness and the integration of the psychic centers within us, on all levels. This is inherently personal and peaceful; an introspective quest of personal learning whether as a solitary or coven member.

The Wiccan Rede

'Eight Words the Wiccan Rede fulfil –
An it harm none, do what thou wilt'

Thus runs the Wiccan Rede, the all encompassing 'Law' governing morality in Wicca. It covers all forms of life; all plants, all animals and all people including ourselves. The Rede assumes total responsibility on the side of the practitioner.
There is, apparently, no documentary evidence that the Rede stems from original historic Pagan times. It does however, appear to be a more recent invention with its first documented publication being in the book entitled, "The Old Laws" by Gerald Gardner, published in 1953.
It is the main tenet and moral code of modern day Wicca and Witchcraft with the word "Rede" being Middle English, meaning 'to give counsel or advice'.

Wicca bestows upon its adherents full responsibility, conscience and judgement for all their actions, hence the emphasis on 'know thyself'. This includes fully understanding where the individual personal boundaries lie. The Wiccan way also encompasses the responsibility to fully accept and work through the Shadow side of ones psyche being our weaknesses and other negative attributes.

It assumes and expects us, as individuals, to be conscious of and work through all unresolved matters in order to become whole and integrated human beings, setting an example and being good role models/ citizens within society. We are therefore bound, in conscience and deed, by the Wiccan Rede as we are responsible to fully comprehend and understand what we are doing, what our intentions are and what the likely outcome will be.

Wicca is a religion of love, personal growth and the veneration of the God and Goddess of Nature, therefore, to be consistent with the Wiccan Rede, our actions seek a positive outcome, a better result for Human kind and Nature. Thus ultimately, responsibility is vested within the individual to understand the inherent morality of the Rede.

Wicca is a way of life which seeks to empower the individual through self-scrutiny, insight and understanding. It is defined more by a can-do, confident and pro-active approach to daily life, rather than fear, a list of prohibitions and sin. Celebrating life's joys and pleasures is as much part of life as is introspection, questioning and being self critical in order to gain wisdom and learn.

Nature's Laws and energies are the properties of the God and Goddess in Wicca. They are the power and the blessing we invoke and work in sympathy with to make our intentions manifest as we work in harmony with Nature's energies and forces, not only for our own spiritual advancement in terms of learning and insight but also to realize visions, goals and ideals through the act of magick and spells.

It is through management, harnessing and manipulating this power and working in sympathy with the dual forces represented in the God and Goddess and the Law of Nature that we enact magick.

Law of Threefold Return

The Law of Three Fold Return is another key principle and moral tenet of modern day Wicca and Witchcraft. Again, there is no documentary proof that it stems from the original Pagan times and, again, the first documentary evidence of this Law is in the writings of Gerald Gardner, although his original source is unknown.

Some sources ascribe the Law of Three-Fold Return to Raymond Buckland as he explains its significance in his book: "Buckland's Complete Book of Witchcraft", {Llewellyn, USA, 1986 - First Edition}. The Law of Three fold Return appears to be more based on the Eastern Principle of the Law of Cause and Effect, called 'Karma'. The word 'Karma' being Sanskrit, meaning 'action', implies that all actions inspire an appropriate reaction, at some stage, whether in this current life, or the next. Implied also is the concept of reincarnation as it presupposes a series of life times in which lessons can be learnt in a spiritual sense, experiences undergone and wrongs made right.

The concept behind the Law of Three-Fold Return is one of doing good and good shall be done back to you, as anything you do shall be returned three fold, whether bad or good, whether in this life time or the next. This Law gives a very strong incentive to always do good and live according to the Wiccan Rede by not harming anyone or anything, as all is alive. It is this concept that acts as a powerful inducement to do our very best, use energies for a positive outcome and generally live a pro-active life and the full integrity expressed in the Wiccan Rede.

This essence of the Wiccan Rede is also encapsulated in another of Wicca's sacred texts which also defines morality and ethics, being the "Charge of the Goddess", written by Doreen Valiente and Gerald Gardner in the early 1950's. An excerpt:

'Keep pure your highest ideals;
strive ever towards them,
let nothing turn you aside.'

NATURE

Often, when we hear about Climate Change and the enhanced Greenhouse Effect, we hear that it is 'Anthropogenic', meaning that it is man-made, differentiating it from the naturally occurring Greenhouse Effect. The naturally occurring Greenhouse Effect is impacted upon and further exacerbated by man's activities such as fossil fuel emissions and forest clearing.

To be sure, floods, storms, disease and drought have been with us right through history. In ancient times, man tried to appease the Gods for their perceived wrath, in many ways including ritual and sacrifice. Our ancestors lived in harmony with Nature's balance and equilibrium, their senses and instincts being in tune with Nature's rhythm and cycles. Therefore, our ancestors' life styles were largely dictated by the forces of nature. Obviously, it is not feasible, nor practicable, or desirable, to return to these ancient practices however, Climate Change is largely predictable and fully understood as being a result of man's lack of respect for the Planet Earth and its context. It is a sign of man's alienation from nature and, also, largely from himself, as he no longer hears his inner voice or sees Nature suffer and being destroyed. The often cited thrust for advancement and progress, appears mostly consumer driven, rather than by a genuine need. It has led to competition, largely driven by man's ego, happily exploited by consumer marketing, all of which in turn has led to the subjugation of Nature, to serve man on his own basis.

This egocentric competitive focus on consumerism and materialism has divorced man from his natural environment, so much so that many children do not know how an egg comes about or how an orange grows. No, today's children grow up largely with only artificial sound and sights largely brought about by electronic media. This has resulted in the last generations growing up *being* entertained, rather than creating their own entertainment and *being* externally stimulated rather than inspiring themselves.

It is rare to find people purposefully planning their days for quiet cerebral study, consciously listening to bird-song and the wind, purposefully looking at the sun and how it courses the sky giving us the seasons, or looking at the direction in which the clouds pass, trying to work out the next weather front. When last have you seen a person scoop up a hand full of soil to smell it, look at its composition and moisture content, or, seen a person study trees and comment on their state of health or critically look at water courses, all in order to read and understand their micro climate and ecology?

This lack of awareness, concern and compassion is a symptom of the mass alienation, which in turn has lead to the parlous state of our environment. Furthermore, the unwillingness of people to critically look at their lifestyles and, yes, even needs, has led man to destroy, whether knowingly or unknowingly, his own context.

The Planet Earth and all it sustains is our habitat. We read and hear that the human enhanced Greenhouse Effect and Global Warming will lead to a rise in sea-level, cause changes in rainfall patterns, greater frequency and intensity of extreme weather conditions such as flooding, droughts, heat-waves and storms. This in turn causes changes in land-use patterns through higher or lower agricultural yields. It also leads to the extinction of species as well as the rise of diseases. Other effects of Global Warming are glacial retreat, reduced summer stream flows and the drying up of wetlands supporting micro-climates and ecosystems. Sharply increased fire danger will cause loss of property and habitat to fauna and flora not to mention loss of life. Global Warming is also responsible for the increased acidification of the oceans and the resulting dying off of coral reefs and marine species.

Scientists have describe the last decade as the warmest on record and most agree that man's activities over the last 50 years are by far the greatest cause of the recent global warming.

In Wicca we seek to live a balanced life, not only through the integration of our own inner Underworld with the Otherworld, but also through an awareness of our way of life, as lived within our context and environment.

We seek to plan our days with meaningful and purposeful activities, which will be beneficial to our environment considering the possible impact of all our actions. This requires a certain level of awareness, focus and a critical approach to our life styles, perceived needs and actions, with the goal being to achieve a balanced way of life in equilibrium with the Divine and Nature.

THE GOD AND GODDESS

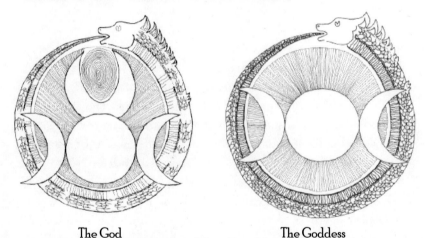

The God   The Goddess

The Symbol of the God and Goddess encircled by the Ouroboros, the symbol of unity, re-creation and infinity.

All religions believe in a Higher Power, a power that is all encompassing and more powerful than us mere mortals living on earth. It is in the manner in which this power is visualized, celebrated and venerated that shows where the main differences in religions lie.

In Wicca we know that there is a Higher Power, an Ultimate Force, the Archetypal Energy, the Supreme Power, because we see it manifest in Nature and within ourselves each and every day.

It must be emphasized that within this work you will find frequent reference to the God and Goddess, angels, teachers and guides and those who lead, teach and guide us. Reference is not being made to physical people resembling us, instead these are energies and forces which we perceive through our own psychic powers using visualization and mental focus. However, entities can make themselves manifest to the schooled few who can see them in a humanoid form. Through our own focussed will, these powers bring about circumstances, states of mind, a series of events or a physical or mental state of being that creates a heightened perception, focus and awareness. This altered state of mind allows us to become acutely aware and receptive as otherwise dormant mental and psychic faculties function to facilitate impressions, experiences and visualizations akin to divine encounters and experiences.

However, in order to make these perceived higher powers more intellectually accessible, comprehendible and even tangible, we make them representative. We personify them and give them names so that during our Rites we may communicate with them. We therefore call them the God and Goddess or Spirit, amongst other names and give them physical representation.
Furthermore, consistent with the Laws of Nature, Wicca, generally identifies the chief Deities as male and female, reflecting the equal power of polarity. The God and Goddess are dynamic and complementary and represent the duality found within nature as well as within our selves.

The God and Goddess are revered and celebrated as a binary team, representing the ultimate power and force. They are celebrated at the Sabbat festivals as complementing each other as the God of the Hunt and the Goddess of Fertility, with the God ruling the dark half of the year, namely from Litha {Midsummer} to Yule {mid Winter}, when the days grow shorter, whilst the Goddess rules the light half of the year, from Yule to Litha, when the days grow longer and warmer.

Historically, this corresponded with Winter and man's dependency on hunting for food at a time when it was too cold for crops to grow, while Spring and Summer were traditionally times for planting and harvesting as it was warmer with longer days.

The Earth, in many traditions, is the predominant realm of the Goddess, for She gives us birth and sustains us in life, however, the life giving qualities of the Earth depend on the warmth and light of the Sun, the realm of the God who complements the Goddess's role. Therefore, the Earth as bearer of all life, subject to the seasons and dependent on the Sun, falls under the rulership of both the God and Goddess in equal power.

As the Earth's cycle reflects the polarity of both the God and Goddess; by Winter and Summer and light and dark, the Moon, as celebrated at Esbats, has always been the full domain of the Goddess. It is visible mainly at night and in ancient times, man perceived it as having a direct effect on life on Earth through its phases, changing tides and effecting the menstrual cycles and fertility of all females. Today we know that the Moon's phases are caused by reflected sunlight however, that has not changed its links with the Goddess with this historic connection being based on its mystical silver glow, its waning and waxing properties, its magnetic qualities; the Moon was the Grand Dame of the Cosmos to our ancestors and as such became a key figure in ancient mythology.

Our legends and myths of ancient times trying to explain phenomena such as Moon cycles and the seasons offer a storehouse of inspiration for most modern Wiccan traditions. They provide analogies and models for seasonal Sabbat themes, such as "The Legend of Persephone" enacted at Mabon {Autumn Equinox}. This rich plethora of ancient legends also inspires and informs many

Pagan traditions regarding their Deities' names and identities as used in ritual and meditations.

Most traditions are also mindful of choosing deity names and identities, which relate to their own culture and that of most of their Coven members. It is a well known fact, that the human Collective Unconscious, as defined by the Swiss Psychologist, Carl Gustav Jung, contains the archetypal symbols, as well as those created by our personal heritage. These symbols relate and correspond to those of the deities and myths created by our own heritage.

Seeing that the working Lunar rituals, or Esbats, aim to generate a group energy within the Coven, it is beneficial that the cultural heritage of the chosen deity pantheon reflects that of the group so that it may do successful energy work. More powerful and sustained energy can be generated if all members can fully relate to the identity of the deity, as a stronger bond through visualization and therefore a deeper understanding, will result.

This may be less important regarding the use of Myths at Sabbats; the solar rituals, as Sabbats are generally more of a celebratory nature, compared to the working lunar Esbat rituals and that most well known myths have, by today, largely transcended cultural boundaries to become general public property.

There are many excellent books on Wicca fully detailing different pantheons and their history, meaning and identities. I have purposefully not given names in the rituals that follow, as the names and identities are unique to each tradition, individual Witch and/or Coven.

However, some popular names used are:

Herne and Epona {English Mythology}, Shiva and Parvati {Hindu}, Odin and Freyja {Norse}, Osiris and Isis {Ancient Egyptian}, Cernunnos and Cerridwen {Celtic}.

Cernunnos and Aradia {Celtic and Italian Witchcraft; Stregharia}

SABBATS AND ESBATS

SABBATS

The book contains celebrations for the eight Sabbats of The Wheel of the Year which I celebrate as they relate to Nature's cycle of the Southern Hemisphere.

For the correspondences to the Northern Hemisphere, please see the following table for approximate dates*.

Sabbat	Northern Hemisphere	Southern Hemisphere
Samhain/Hallowe'en	October 31- 1 November	April 30-1 May
Yule/Winter Solstice	Between 20-23 December	Between 20-23 June
Imbolc /The Quickening	January 31-1 February	July 31- 1 August
Ostara/ Spring Equinox	Between 20-23 March	Between 20-23 September
Beltane/ Festival of the Flowering	April 30-1 May	October 31-1 November
Litha/Midsummer	Between 20-23 June	Between 20-23 December
Lughnasadh/Harvest Festival	July 31 - 1 August	January 31- 1 February
Mabon/Autumn Equinox	Between 20-23 September	Between 20-23 March

*Please consult a current Astrological diary to confirm correct dates.

The Sabbats, relating to the position of the Sun to the Horizon and giving us our seasons are commonly divided into the Greater Sabbats and the Lesser Sabbats. The Greater Sabbats, also known as the Cross-Quarter days mark the mid points between the Solstices and the Equinoxes. The Lesser Sabbats are the two Solstices and the two Equinoxes, also known as the Quarter days. Together, the eight days of festival celebrate life on the land, the Earth in relation to the Sun and Moon as well as the animal and plant realms. All Sabbats are also known as Fire Festivals and in ritual, they were also celebrated with bonfires to mark the celebration of the sun and its life giving light and warmth, or the dissipation thereof, as reflected in the seasons.

The Sabbats were historically celebrated closest to Full Moon where possible.

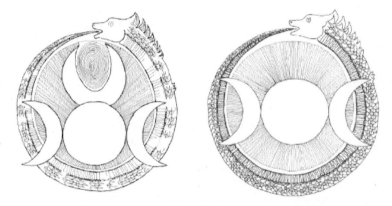

The Greater Sabbats in the Northern Hemisphere are:

- Historically, **Samhain** is celebrated at the beginning of November, as fodder was running low for the cattle due to the onset of winter, heralding the time to slaughter any animals unlikely to survive the long and cold winter.
- **Imbolc**, beginning of February signaled the birth of the first lambs.
- **Beltane** was the time of mating and clearing of pests from animals by passing them through or between the fires.
- **Lughnasadh**, beginning of August, marked the first harvest for storage.

The Lesser Sabbats, the Solstices and the Equinoxes are:

- Yule, the Winter Solstice
- Ostara, Spring Equinox
- Litha, Summer Solstice
- Mabon, Autumn Equinox

The Sabbats also celebrate the balanced interlinking between the male principle as symbolized by the Sun; the God and female principle as symbolized by the Earth; the Goddess. Mythologically, they celebrated the binary and polar forces of the God and Goddess.

The Eight Sabbats as depicted by the eight spoked Wheel of the Year symbol tells us the life story of the God and Goddess. It is the story of the God as the Sun God, consort to the Goddess, as the Earth and consistent with the Laws of Nature and Wiccan philosophy the Wheel of the Year forms the story of birth, life, death and rebirth, the Cycle of Infinity and Reincarnation with the seasonal cycle acting as the metaphor for the regeneration of life.

The Wheel of the Year is seen as being divided up into two halves, one is the light half of the year and the other is the dark half of the year, with Yule and Litha marking the division. This signifies the waxing year, from Winter Solstice {Yule} to Midsummer {Litha} as the days grow longer, and the waning half of the year, from Litha to Yule, as the days grow shorter.

Some traditions see the division between Samhain and Beltane, where the God and Goddess court at Beltane and couple in the Grand Rite at Samhain, giving birth to the Sun Child at Yule. In terms of the Laws of Nature, it makes more sense to me personally that Yule marks the birth of the Divine Child as Sun King, with the Sun King's or Corn King's sacrifice at Lughnasadh; the first harvest. The latter division contains the three waxing year Sabbats being Imbolc, Ostara and Beltane and the three waning year Sabbats, with Lughnasadh {Harvest Festival}, Mabon and Samhain.

During the dark half of the year, the Northern Hemisphere Winter, the God is celebrated as the Holly King because Holly is an evergreen and a tree that seemed to our ancestors to have never died during the cold winter months. During this dark half, the God is also celebrated as the Lord of the Hunt.

During the light half of the year, he is celebrated as the Oak King, as a deciduous tree which comes to life with new green growth in Spring. He is also celebrated as the Corn King, Lord of the Harvest, consort to the Goddess; the Goddess of Fertility and the Earth, ensuring good crop yields.

In some traditions, the light half of the year is celebrated as the Lady of the Harvest when the Goddess rules as the Earth bringing forth bountiful crops.

The dark half of the year is then celebrated as the Lord of the Hunt, as during Winter the Earth 'recovers', when ancient man was dependent on hunting for food.

 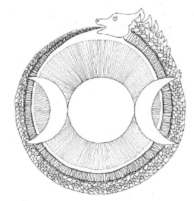

The Sabbat Wheel of the Year
Northern Hemisphere

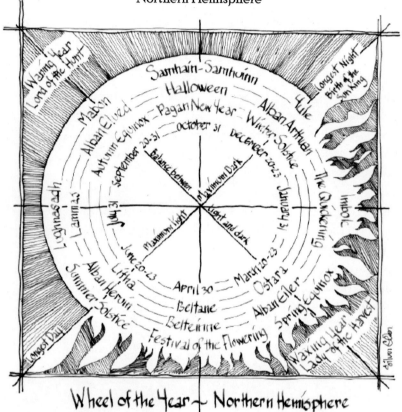

Wheel of the Year — Northern Hemisphere

The God's Life Cycle

Briefly, the life cycle of the God as celebrated on the Sabbats, evolves thus:

- Our God is born as the Sun Child at Yule as it is the Mid-Winter turning point when the days start to grow longer.
- The young boy grows and undergoes his first initiation at Imbolc, The Quickening. It is the time of the thaw and the promise of new life as the Sun's strength grows, melting the ice.
- At Ostara, the God as a young man and adolescent, Lord of the

18

Greenwood, comes into maturity and meets the Goddess.

■ At Beltane the God and Goddess couple, although he does not stay with her. The God takes on the shepherd role.

The Sabbat Wheel of the Year
Southern Hemisphere

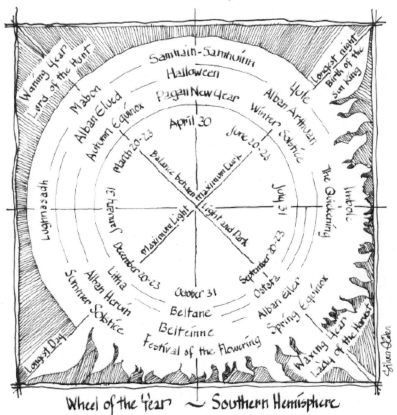

Wheel of the Year ～ Southern Hemisphere

■ Litha celebrates the marriage of the God and Goddess as she is pregnant. Great change comes over the God as he takes on full responsibility as husband and as the Sun King ruling over the land as consort to the Goddess. He is at his prime physically and in terms of status. They both oversee abundance and growth.

■ Lughnasadh marks the sacrifice of the God as Corn King at first harvest. He loses strength as the corn seeds and fruit drop and the nights grow longer. The God begins his decent into the Underworld.

■ At Mabon, the God as King of the Underworld briefly returns to Earth to capture the Goddess, as the onset of winter visibly manifests in the Autumn/Fall and the life force drains from the Earth.

■ At Samhain, both the God and Goddess rule the Underworld as equals where they give each other the divine Gift of knowledge and insight. The God rises to the realm of Spirit, the Supreme Godhead while the Goddess, in her role as Goddess of Fertility, is pregnant with the Divine Child, the Sun Child to be born at Yule.

This completes the Wheel of the Year and thus recommences the Cycle of birth, life, death and rebirth at the following Yule.

The correlation of the opposite of each festival as they are arranged on the Wheel emphasize the recurring theme of birth, life, death, rebirth:

■ The two Solstices symbolize birth, life, regeneration and the dawning of new beginnings in that the seed symbolically falls at Midsummer/ Litha heralding the waning year to be reborn as the sun child at Yule.

■ The two Equinoxes while symbolizing the balance between light and dark, symbolize formation, creation of Spring/ Ostara and the consolidation and introspection at Autumn/ Mabon. The learning experience, experimentation and adventure having taken place at Spring is further considered, assessed and emotionally and mentally processed at Mabon – the introspected harvesting and storing of the conclusions reached of one's life as the days shorten and the sun sets.

■ The dynamic between Samhain and Beltane is most strongly symbolized by creation, sexuality, fertility, sowing, planting and generation versus the harvesting, reaping and death with the promise of rebirth. This polarity comes closest to the Eastern concept of 'Karma': the polarity of action and reaction in the maxim of "what we plant, we shall reap". It also expresses the concept of what we invoke, shall manifest.

■ The polarity of Imbolc and Lughnasadh is one of innocence and first initiation versus responsibility, experience and knowledge acquired through experience. Parallels can also be drawn between the innocence of childhood and the responsibility of adult life; of free adventure by the unrestrained soul versus the binds and limitations imposed by responsibility and implementation of experience gained.

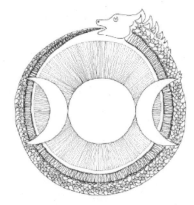

ESBATS

As we have discussed, Sabbats are the celebrations of life and the Wheel of the Year, the Esbats are the working meetings of Witches. They are often held at each Moon phase, notably at each Full Moon and at Dark Moon.

Lunar Calender

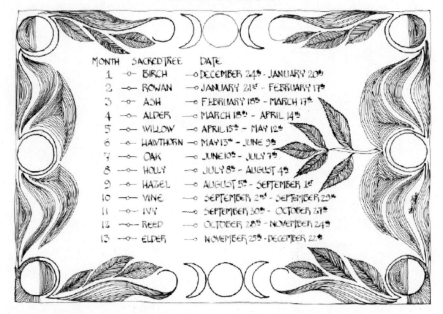

MONTH	SACRED TREE	DATE
1	BIRCH	DECEMBER 24th – JANUARY 20th
2	ROWAN	JANUARY 21st – FEBRUARY 17th
3	ASH	FEBRUARY 18th – MARCH 17th
4	ALDER	MARCH 18th – APRIL 14th
5	WILLOW	APRIL 15th – MAY 12th
6	HAWTHORN	MAY 13th – JUNE 9th
7	OAK	JUNE 10th – JULY 7th
8	HOLLY	JULY 8th – AUGUST 4th
9	HAZEL	AUGUST 5th – SEPTEMBER 1st
10	VINE	SEPTEMBER 2nd – SEPTEMBER 29th
11	IVY	SEPTEMBER 30th – OCTOBER 27th
12	REED	OCTOBER 28th – NOVEMBER 24th
13	ELDER	NOVEMBER 25th – DECEMBER 22nd

Depending on circumstance, your own personal commitment as a Solitary, the structure of your Coven, or if you run a teaching Grove, meetings are also held at waning and waxing Moon, known as the Quarter Moons. In this manner there would be a meeting each week, making up the 28 day lunar cycle.

The Full Moon is the time for energy work, for magic and healing, whether done as a solitary Witch or with a Coven. It is the time when the Moon's energies are at their greatest and most palpable. However, if there is no urgent work to be done, it is also a powerful time for divination and/ or meditation.

There are Thirteen Full Moons in each Lunar year as the Lunar calendar differs from our every day Gregorian calendar by starting around Yule/Litha or the 22-23rd December and ending on the 24th December. The Lunar Cycle is only 28 or 29 days long giving us thirteen Full Moons.

I celebrate each Full Moon for which I have written my own personal version of the Charge of the Goddess, the Great Mother Charge. I have also included Charges for the Waxing and Waning Moon; the First and Third Quarter, with the Maiden Mother Charge being applicable for the First Quarter and the Crone Charge for the Third Quarter. The Triple Goddess Charge or The Charge of the Enchantress is used for the Dark Moon or New Moon.

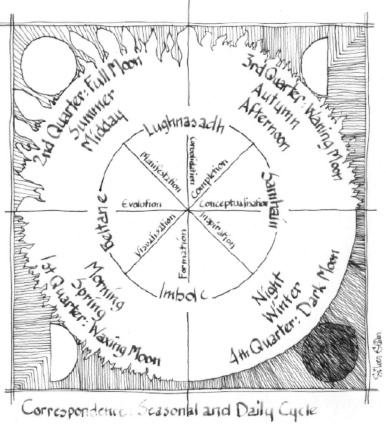

Correspondence: Seasonal and Daily Cycle

The phases of the Moon with their energies and symbolism form a microcosm of the entire annual seasonal cycle and the microcosm for each daily cycle:

I have included Meditations for the Waning and Waxing Quarter with topics relating to the qualities of the energies of growth and dissipation.

I have purposefully not covered Spells and Healing, as this work is unique and personal to each individual Witch and/ or Coven.

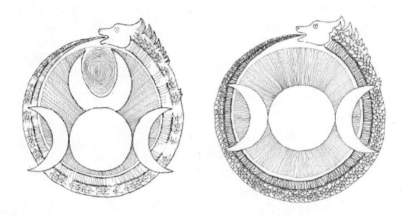

WICCA, PAGANISM AND COSMOLOGY

In modern Wicca today, many traditions borrow cosmologies from other religions in order to form a new unique graphic structure; a road map if you like, by which to guide religious practice. These include the Kabbalistic Tree of Life, the OTz ChIIM, {pronounced: ah-yetz chayim} as contained in the Sepher ha-Zohar, or, the 'Book of Splendor' which is one of the major source works of Kabbalistic literature of the Jewish Esoteric Tradition or Hebrew Mysticism.

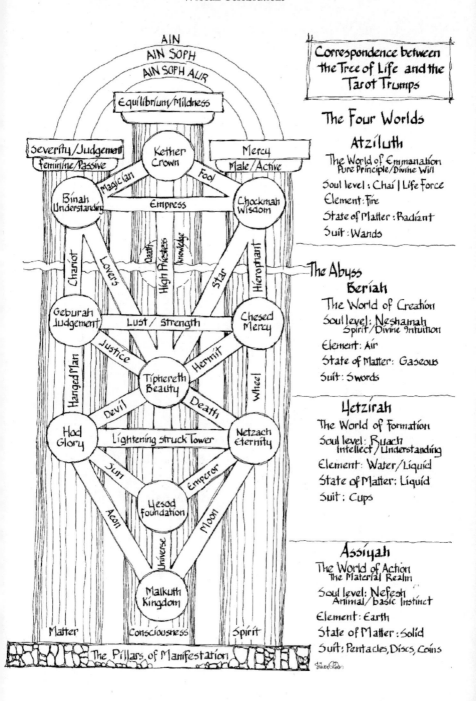

AIN
AIN SOPH
AIN SOPH AUR

Equilibrium/Mildness

Severity/Judgement
feminine/Passive

Kether
Crown

Mercy
Male/Active

Binah
Understanding

Magician

Empress

Fool

Chockmah
Wisdom

Chariot

Lovers

Death
High Priestess

Knowledge

Star

Hierophant

Geburah
Judgement

Lust / Strength

Chesed
Mercy

Hanged Man

Justice

Tiphereth
Beauty

Hermit

Wheel

Devil

Death

Hod
Glory

Lightening struck Tower

Netzach
Eternity

Sun

Emperor

Yesod
Foundation

Aeon

Moon

Universe

Malkuth
Kingdom

Spirit

Matter

Consciousness

The Pillars of Manifestation

Correspondence between the Tree of Life and the Tarot Trumps

The Four Worlds

Atziluth

The World of Emmanation
Pure Principle/Divine Will

Soul level : Chai | Life Force

Element: Fire

State of Matter : Radiant

Suit : Wands

The Abyss

Beriah

The World of Creation

Soul level: Neshamah
Spirit/Divine Intuition

Element: Air

State of Matter: Gaseous

Suit: Swords

Yetzirah

The World of Formation

Soul level: Ruach
Intellect/Understanding

Element: Water/Liquid

State of Matter: Liquid

Suit: Cups

Assiyah

The World of Action
The Material Realm

Soul level: Nefesh
Animal/basic Instinct

Element: Earth

State of Matter: Solid

Suit: Pentacles, Discs, Coins

The Tree itself forms a diagram depicting ten centers of activity, or states of being, called the Sephiroth (singular: Sephira) arranged on three columns connected by twenty two paths, forming a glyph. Visualizing the glyph in front of you the columns are arranged with the Pillar of Severity on the left; the Pillar of Equilibrium in the center and the Pillar of Mercy to the right. The twenty-two paths, incidentally, corresponding to the 22 Major Arcana of the Tarot deck, display options or directions of the ten states of being by which one could navigate life's journey. In this way, the glyph acts as a map for the individual to find a path towards union with the Divine.

The Three Worlds

The original Pagan vision of the Cosmos which also abides by the occult axiom: 'As above, so below' is that of the Three Worlds: The Underworld, the Middleworld and the Otherworld or Overworld. In ancient times, the Underworld related to the home of our ancestors, the Spiritworld. In modern day psychology Carl Gustav Jung related the Underworld to our Collective Unconscious containing symbolism of an archetypal nature transcending cultural, racial and even geographic boundaries. The Underworld is also symbolic of the deep dark shadow side within ourselves. This is the realm of the Dark Goddess leading you to your true Self; the Goddess of Witchcraft who encourages you to find your true Soul and identity.

The Middelworld forms the material realm of all living beings, the realm of living experience, including us, our mortal selves on Earth. This realm corresponds to Jung's paradigm of our everyday thought via the conscious brain.

The Otherworld, or Overworld, relates to the realm of the Gods, corresponding to Jung's concept of the personal unconscious. This realm is, in some Traditions, further divided into two realms, being one of Enlightenment and the other being that of the Supreme

Godhead, the latter being referred to in Jungian Psychology as the Superconscious, the Unknowable Divine Self.

In ancient Norse mythology, Yggdrasil, the World Tree was believed to form the central axis of the world, the Axis Mundi, forming the connection between the Underworld, the Middleworld and the Otherworld. The World Tree's roots dwelt in the Underworld while its trunk stood in the Middleworld and its branches reached out and up into the Otherworld. Similarly, certain creatures became symbols of the different realms, such as the snake symbolizing a chthonic, or underworld, creature seen living in underground burrows; it therefore was seen to be an Underworld creature. Most other animals dwelt above ground; they, like human beings were creatures of the Middleworld, whilst birds, living in the World Tree's branches were seen to be inhabitants and creatures of the Otherworld.

Yggdrasil, the World Tree therefore gave a physical manifestation of the Hermetic or magical axiom: 'As above, so below' and like the World Tree we clearly visualize the Three Worlds when we stand within our magical Circle. We cast the Circle and set out the Elemental candles on the appropriate compass points and see the Elemental Realms of Earth, Air, Water and Fire as they form part of the Material or Physical Realm of the Earth, also known as the Middleworld. The Elements are the Four States of Matter that allow life to take place; that sustain life in the physical realm of Earth itself.

The magic Circle represents in microcosm format, the macrocosm of which we are part. Inside the Circle we form the conduit and connection between the Worlds as we practice; as we tune in on different levels.

We visualize the Otherworld above us with the realm of the Gods, we perceive the Underworld below us and see and sense the Elemental Realms in the Middleworld around us on the Earth Plane.

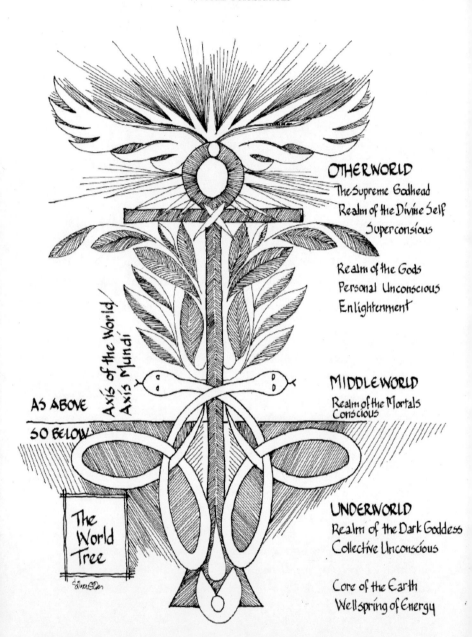

OTHERWORLD
The Supreme Godhead
Realm of the Divine Self
Superconsious

Realm of the Gods
Personal Unconscious
Enlightenment

MIDDLEWORLD
Realm of the Mortals
Conscious

UNDERWORLD
Realm of the Dark Goddess
Collective Unconscious

Core of the Earth
Wellspring of Energy

AS ABOVE

SO BELOW

Axis of the World
Axis Mundi

The
World
Tree

This corresponds to the practice of placing the Altar in the center
of the Circle, at which you conduct ritual: under the light of the
Supreme Godhead, the highest power of all Worlds. This is the

connection to Spirit, via the Three Worlds, which is also the key goal in raising power within the Circle, often referred to as the 'Cone of Power' visualized as forming an apex above the Circle center, below which the Altar is located and the Rite is conducted. We form the fulcrum, symbolically and metaphorically, as we stand at the Altar in the physical Middleworld and the Earthly realm. This visualization corresponds to the psychological alignment of practicing Magick and conducting spiritual work requiring all aspects of the psyche and all levels of awareness to be used. The cosmological paradigm of the Three Worlds is the graphic visualization or road map, if you like, to any form of spiritual work and the wish to manifest thought forms in Otherworld realms.

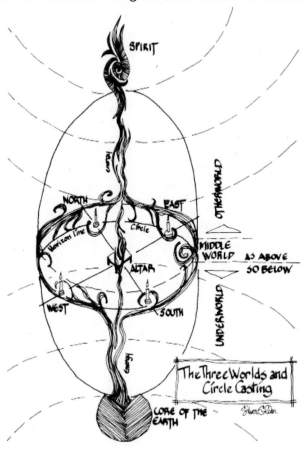

Wicca, also known as the Old Religion, being Pagan in origin, is not a practice of dogma and doctrine. Instead, practice and worship takes place within a framework of cult acts and ritual designed to make manifest the experience of the Divine. Nature and its energies is the vehicle through which the direct contact with deity takes place, as all of Nature is alive and sacred and there is life in All. Wicca and Paganism see all of life as having a common origin. Today's Science has proven this through the Big Bang Theory with overwhelming consensus within the scientific community being that the Big Bang did happen.

The Big Bang took place approximately 13.7 Billion years ago when there was no matter, no time and no space, as we understand them today. 13.7 Billion years ago our Universe began as a seething mass of energy, smaller than an egg. Within a fraction of second, this pure energy exploded into matter and eventually grew large enough to encompass All That Is.

The Universe is ever expanding and speeding up in motion. The matter created was Hydrogen and Helium; the building blocks of our stars and galaxies.

Hydrogen is the most important Element of the Chemical Elements and the Periodic Table, comprising 75% of the Elemental Mass of the Universe. It is present in water and in most organic compounds. Water as we know, is essential to all forms of life. It is comprised of two hydrogen atoms and one oxygen atom {H_2O}. About 70% of the mass of our bodies is made up of water.

Hydrogen is present in most organic compounds meaning, any number of a large class of chemical compounds are comprised of molecules containing carbon and hydrogen. These include compounds of prime importance to Biochemistry, such as Vitamins, Proteins, Peptides, Amino-acids, Enzymes and Hormones, to name just a few. As mentioned, Hydrogen, the key building block of the stars and our galaxies is, therefore, also the principle agent of all life on the Earth.

This was the formation of the Divine Source of All Life. All is

30

alive and in constant motion and we, like all forms of life, bear the Blueprint of this primordial origin. As demonstrated, we contain atoms created 13.7 Billion years ago. We are part of the Universe in origin and evolution as we are made up of water and are thereby subject to all the energies of the Universe, as is the Earth with its oceans, lakes, rivers and all other water bodies.

We are part of this ever expanding energy field and are therefore subject to its powers and influences. The ancient Pagans, as we do in Wicca today, understood that we share this common origin. We believe this to be the Divine Spark within us. We believe that through focused thought and will, we can harness these residual energies within us that correspond in vibration to the energies outside of us, to make manifest changes on Earth that could bring about an improved situation, however big or small, in our daily material existence. This is what we understand as the enactment of Magick.

Ritual and the performance of cult acts provide the vehicle and framework to create an altered state of mind and heighten the senses in order to directly experience deity, for a variety of purposes, i.e: the performance of mediumship. Paganism and Wicca accept and affirm a direct link and connection between the Divine and humanity. Deity is fundamentally imminent or indwelling in all forms of life, including ourselves.

Paganism and Wicca affirm that there is also a direct link between this material world in which we live and the Otherworld or, the Outer Realms. The concept of re-incarnation teaches us that we evolve and regenerate and the Otherworld represents the transformation of our physical selves. It is the Soul or, the Spirit body that transcends the earthly physical realm to be re-manifest within the cycle of birth, life, death and re-birth.

The Cosmos is seen as the extension of the Earth and Nature; the All Encompassing context in which transpersonal exchange with

Deity occurs. Nature and the Cosmos also provide the setting in which direct contact with the Divine occurs, via a mutual interdependence between us as humans and the Otherworld, of which we see ourselves as an integral part. A life of equilibrium between the material mundane world and the sacred and spiritual realm is the key goal of life as a Pagan. This is manifest in the practice of the religion whereby a dynamic exchange between the Spiritual and material world takes place within Nature and its energies as a facilitator.

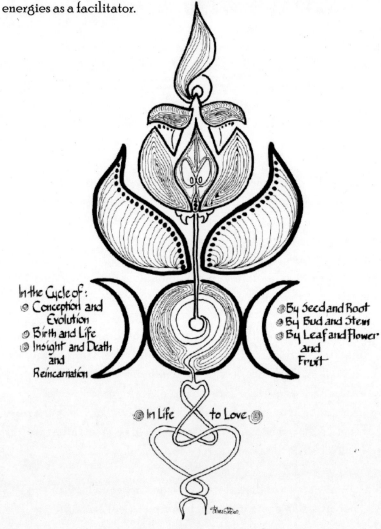

In the Cycle of:
- Conception and Evolution
- Birth and Life
- Insight and Death and Reincarnation

- By Seed and Root
- By Bud and Stem
- By Leaf and Flower and Fruit

In Life to Love

THE UNDERWORLD

In Wicca, the Underworld is defined in many different ways and has several different meanings, the predominant meaning being the quest for Light within the Darkness, knowledge within ignorance and of the Unconscious mind. This leads to the fully integrated Self, as will be discussed later.

One thing it certainly is NOT – The Underworld is not Hell as defined by the Christian Church or any other sense. Wicca does not recognize a Hell.

Wicca, instead believes in reincarnation, in that we as individuals evolve in wisdom, as we dance the Spiral Dance of birth, life, death and rebirth.

The Underworld is also the core feature of most Myths, as the place where our Ancestors dwell and new insights and wisdoms are won, symbolized by the Holy Grail, usually achieved through some form of initiation by overcoming the dark side of ourselves, in order to grow in wisdom.

In Wicca we seek to become fully integrated human beings through learning about ourselves, our full potential, all aspects of our psyches, in order to be aware and harness all possible abilities and talents we may have. We do this by learning from the Principles of Nature as they manifest in our everyday lives as our Great Spiritual Teacher. It is a well known scientific fact that we only use a fraction of our brain capacity in our daily lives, notably the conscious brain, ruled by our Ego.

It is well worth noting here that our lives are in many ways governed more by societal norms and customs, satisfying expectations and being entertained by external stimuli such as TV, all of which are ruled by the conscious brain and the ego. This is very different to a life that is informed by intuition, introspection, psychic perception and seeking stimuli within oneself. Obviously a balance needs to be found.

However, when we dream, it is the unconscious brain that communicates with us through the use of analogy, symbolism and metaphor. This is the realm of the Underworld; the Collective Unconscious as defined by modern day Psychology, notably that of Carl Gustav Jung.

The unconscious brain is not ruled by the Ego and as such is 'entirely honest' or non-critical. Often the depiction and rendition of its message, in the form of dream symbols can appear, at times, to be rather bizarre or frightening. The process of Integration, as defined by Jung, is to achieve a level of proficiency whereby the unconscious brain can readily communicate with the conscious brain, without the Ego interfering and filtering out essential information which we rationally feel uncomfortable with. Full integration, as we seek to achieve in Wicca, requires total honesty and an unbiased approach to ourselves and within ourselves. It is through this integration, the unfiltered constant flow of information, no matter how uncomfortable its message may appear on the surface, between the unconscious brain and the conscious that enables us to grow, as people with true insight, empathy and real understanding.

The acceptance of the unconscious brain, its symbols and its messages in an unprejudiced manner, without the ego having censored unpalatable information, is a key step to Wicca's quest for personal growth.

The Divide

When we start to work with the dark world of the Underworld; the Collective Unconscious and its symbols via personal dream analysis we are said to be crossing the Divide. Apart from defining the different Worlds and the different Planes within each World, the Divide is the Metaphoric liminal boundary between the different realms of the Psyche and Consciousness. We cross the Divide at night to access our Collective Unconscious as we move from our conscious analytical thought process, through sleep, via the subconscious, over the Divide into the realms of the unconscious, in our dreams. Here we receive messages in symbol laden dream form, which we hope to carry through to our conscious mind, uncensored, to awaken the next morning, just that little wiser. We have crossed the Divide, on a personal level and are said to be Between the Worlds, of our psyches, within ourselves in order to create a Whole, the fully integrated individual.

The same symbolism occurs and is relevant when we enact ritual within our magic Circle where the Divide is the threshold Between the Worlds; the boundary between this earthly material world and the Otherworld. We cross the Divide into a neutral time and space referred to when, in ritual we say:

"This is a time that is not a time, in a place that is not a place, on a day that is not a day,
we stand at the threshold between the Worlds,
before the veil of Mysteries"

The Circle thus defines the neutral area where energies can be generated and links with the other worlds and outer realms created, established and defined.

This will be explained more fully later.

The Anima, the Animus and the Divine within us

A further key concept of the psyche is the Anima and Animus, as defined by Jung. The Anima is the latent feminine aspect within a man's psyche, while the Animus is the latent male attribute of the woman's psyche. Often these are represented as a wise woman in a dream of a man, or an older man in a dream of a woman. They can communicate via spoken words in a dream, if you remember the words the next day. These figures manifest in the unconscious mind and the Underworld of us all and are key advisors guiding us as individuals. The more proficient we become in our personal dream analysis the more able we are to quickly discern the individual roles each figure plays within our dreams. While the Anima and the Animus are nearly always the opposite sex to the dreamer, they need not be elderly; they could also be young, or even children, and there could be more than one, but they always have an important message in a dream. It is important then to capture the message without any interference from the rational conscious brain, the Ego, to be useful. Many Witches keep a *dream diary* as part of their ongoing quest for integration.

Let us return to the God and Goddess, our dynamic and complementary binary team. If we accept our lives as a cycle of birth, life, death and rebirth symbolized as the Spiral Dance, we accept that we undergo this cycle on a daily basis; in the function of our minds, in the conscious mind during the day, passing through from the subconscious and into the unconscious, at night. Here we cross the psychological Divide, passing through the Gates and beyond the Veil into the deepest recesses of our own Unconscious mind, seeking integration, as we cast that Veil aside.

Such is the cycle the God undergoes at Litha, when he realizes that there is another side to him, a whole different aspect to him as symbolized by his marriage to the Goddess, his Anima.

His strength fails him at Lughnasadh, when he is sacrificed as the corn ripens for the first harvest and he passes, symbolically, from the subconscious to the unconscious where he is to become the Dark Lord of the Underworld. The unconscious is also known as the Dark World because it is relatively unknown, as we think during the day with only our rational conscious mind and the unconscious only activates at night, in our sleep, via dreams.

At Mabon, the God briefly comes back to Earth to capture the Goddess and take her to the Underworld with him. Here she gives him the Gift of Insight. Symbolically, the God is coming to terms with his unconscious mind while he dwells in the Underworld. He captures the Goddess who opens up the realms of the Anima within his psyche. She brings to light his feminine side, the gift of feeling, of emotion, intuition, empathy, sensuality, sensitivity and yes, psychic abilities too. These are the hidden resources latent within a man, largely covered up by societal norms and image.

At Samhain, the God and Goddess share the Underworld throne, symbolically and metaphorically as fully integrated individuals, sharing their masculine and feminine consciousness in full understanding, acceptance and function.
For a more rational approach, we could say that the Anima and Animus within us, for we do have both, except that the opposite sex predominates, representing the God and Goddess within us.

Once we have achieved a certain level of integration, we find that not a day goes by without a quiet word, a short film clip type vision, a sense, a feeling, a sudden awareness happening within us at any time of the day or night. These messages originate within the psyche; from our Super conscious or our Divine Selves for we are part of the greater Whole; the Cosmos and of Matter and as such, carry within us the accumulated wisdom of our ancestors and incarnations. We are part of this large energy field and therefore subject to its vibrations, its ebb and flow where thoughts resonate on different planes. As we accept this and open up ourselves to this vast etheric realm we develop the sensitivity enabling us to send and receive thought forms, messages, images, feelings and emotions. This is the essence of Magick, the Craft side of Wicca, as a magical mystical religion.

Depending on how proficient we are, we need not wait until we sleep to access this endless realm of unharnessed wisdom and insight of the Underworld. We do this via deep meditation, path-working and visualization. It's a matter of how well we focus, visualize and tune out all other stimuli until we feel, see, hear and even smell the primordial nothingness before we embark on our journey across the Divide of our psyches and realms.

To return to the discussion of Past Lives, it is easy to accept that much of this wealth of knowledge we carry within us, in symbol and metaphor form, derives from past incarnations and that within each life we add to this vast reservoir only to re-enter it in each subsequent incarnation. It is also easy to visualize that we may have learnt skills and achieved abilities in past incarnations, which we rediscover in subsequent incarnations; they are the natural gift or talent, the uncanny ease and proficiency in a certain field or skill. This is where we could hear statements made like: "You must have been a Doctor in a Past Life!" as we observe the love and dedication, the calling and natural skill with the deepest sense of reward within the practitioner.

THE OTHERWORLD

Lets briefly return to the Norse Mythological World Tree, Yggdrasil; symbolizing the Axis Mundi or World Axis by bridging the Divide between the Worlds, the Underworld, the Middleworld and the Otherworld or Overworld. While the World Tree, Yggdrasil, symbolizes the Macrocosm around us, the metaphor also holds true, symbolically, for our personal quest for insight and integration as we seek to integrate the realms of our psyches.

On a personal level we can equate ourselves with Yggdrasil by having our roots in the Underworld gaining nourishing insight from the Unconscious mind, with its rich symbolism and metaphor which we glean through dreams and which we draw into our conscious mind to inform our daily lives.
The other half of our tree reaches through the Middleworld, the earthly material realm, to the Otherworld, outside of ourselves, the

endless planes of coursing energy of the Greater Universe, the All of which we are a part of physically, mentally and spiritually. It can be said, seeing that nature manifests itself as polarity, that the Unconscious of the Dark World, is located within ourselves and the Otherworld is the light world, outside ourselves. The Underworld makes up our own personal mysteries of our inner world and the Otherworld being the mysteries of our Outerworld and Conscious mind.

The union of both, which is our quest in Wicca, forms the Whole in Microcosm, the integrated Self, like our personal Yggdrasil growing in the field.

The Otherworld and the Four Planes

The Otherworld is often visualized as being comprised of four planes, in some cases more, but the four planes are the most common visualization. It must be added that these are not to be seen as layers but more as realms, fields, expanses which overlap, intersect and are in constant motion, moving around one another. All can be accessed at any time, and in some cases, simultaneously. They are:

The Physical Material Plane
Our Earth, equated with the Middleworld of Norse mythology, is where we live in the here and now in our current life.

The Astral Plane
The Plane of the Stars, as derived from Latin with 'Astrum', meaning Star, is also known as the Plane of the Gods. This Plane we are likely to visit most often, with its sub-planes and realms, through dreams, meditations and via projection in its many forms. This is the realm where most of our magic work is created, formed and projected, and in some instances, manifest. This is also the realm, with its many sub-realms, where most of the Spiritual entities abide, eg: The Nature

Spirits, also called the Elementals. It's the home of our Summerland and its processes of reincarnation. It's also the locus of the Akashic Records; Sanskrit for Records of Spirit- namely the records of our Past, Present and Future. The Astral Plane is also known as the Ethereal Plane.

The Mental Plane

This is the Spiritual Connection between our Mind and the Otherworld. It is another realm we are likely to visit reasonably often, as the realm where many of our ideas and concepts for magic work are born. It is also known as the Upper Astral Plane and is the realm of thought-forms and thoughts, where intent is conceptualized to be created and manifest in the Astral and Physical plane.

The Spiritual Plane

This is the Realm of the Pure Enlightenment and Insight, the Realm of the Supreme Godhead and The All. This is the realm of the God and Goddess. We do not normally gain access here.

These realms and planes are better understood as states of Being, states of Experience and different stages and states of Enlightenment as we learn about ourselves, our locus within the Cosmos as well as our past, present and future.

Generally, these planes are accessed, mainly in Meditation, via our will and strength of visualization, created by our mind via the indwelling Divine, with a clear concept of the loci we wish to see and visit. Our mind and Soul is our link to both worlds, the Underworld and the Otherworld, making us a whole human being. Our brain is the physical functioning organ inside our skull while the mind, is a function of the brain.

The realms can be further visualized as being made up of all

encompassing and enveloping Ether and non material energy
fields that vibrate, pulsate and move at different frequencies which
are in constant motion. They are vibrations of heat, magnetism,
electricity and light, forever coursing and traversing all realms,
hence our potential to be in communication via an infinite resource
of energy to access knowledge and information about different
aspects of our Selves. Our own Self has many different identities, in
the same way as we have different guides and teachers protecting
and guiding us. These guides and teachers are not physical people
or humanoid but different forms of energies interacting on the
higher realms. They could also be better understood as our 'instincts'.
They are also understood as a higher aspect of ourselves as well
as being visualized as energy fields that manifest depending on
requirements and circumstances.

Firstly, one aspect is our Astral Self, the self that communes on
the Astral Plane and all its sub-planes, the Mental Self, often
called the Higher Self, creates the thought-forms on the Mental
Plane through the Spiritual Self as it communes directly with the
Supreme Godhead; our God and Goddess. These identities can be
interchanged any time as we traverse the planes through our inner
mind's eye and requirements change.

If we accept that the forces of Nature and the Cosmos, the
infinite and Ever-changing Universe are manifest and to us,
comprehendible as vibrating energy planes comprising of heat,
electricity, light and magnetism with Ether as a vehicle, it is
not difficult to understand how these can interact with the Four
Elements to make thought-forms manifest. Seeing that our bodies
are largely comprised of water and that our motor control is
governed by electrical impulses, it is also not hard to see how energy
around us affects us, and how through power of the mind, we are
capable of forming a connection between ourselves and the higher
planes. In the end, we are part of this greater whole as a product of
the Divine Source of All Things, being our own microcosmic energy

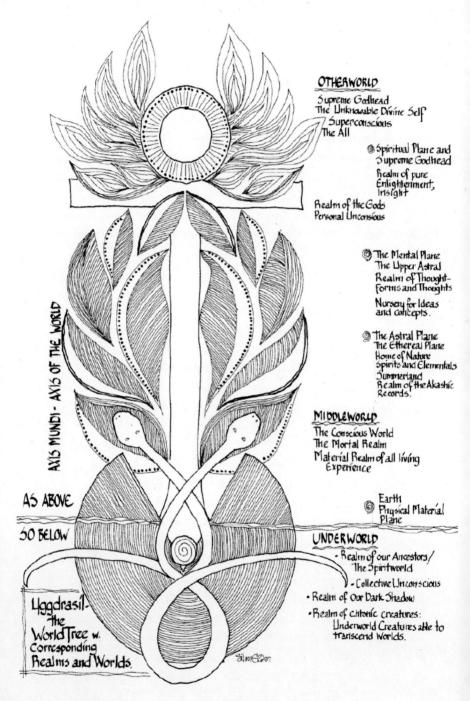

OTHERWORLD
Supreme Godhead
The Unknowable Divine Self
Superconscious
The All

Spiritual Plane and
Supreme Godhead
Realm of pure
Enlightenment,
Insight
Realm of the Gods
Personal Unconscious

The Mental Plane
The Upper Astral
Realm of Thought-
forms and Thoughts

Nursery for Ideas
and Concepts.

The Astral Plane
The Ethereal Plane
Home of Nature
Spirits and Elementals
Summerland
Realm of the Akashic
Records.

MIDDLEWORLD
The Conscious World
The Mortal Realm
Material Realm of all living
Experience

Earth
Physical Material
Plane

UNDERWORLD
- Realm of our Ancestors/
The Spiritworld
- Collective Unconscious
- Realm of Our Dark Shadow
- Realm of chtonic creatures:
Underworld Creatures able to
transcend Worlds.

AXIS MUNDI - AXIS OF THE WORLD

AS ABOVE

SO BELOW

Yggdrasil-
the
World Tree w.
Corresponding
Realms and Worlds.

field, interacting with the energy fields of the All. We are therefore subject to all its forces.

One way in which the Divine Spark manifests on the earthly physical realm is through our Auras, the field of force that surrounds our Astral body, as it uses our physical body as a vehicle on Earth. The Aura reflects our state of mind, stage of enlightenment, emotions and physical health through the display of luminous radiance pulsating and emanating from us in the radiant colors of the rainbow created by different vibrational frequencies.

Before we attempt any access to the higher planes in the form of Astral Travel, I suggest you note the following:
■　　Provided our intent is one of light, learning, insight and Spiritual advancement and all Craft work we do, is for the Highest ideals and purest causes, full protection will readily be afforded to us by our higher powers at all times.
■　　The Astral body, normally residing within our living physical body on Earth, is also linked to us via the *"Silver Cord"*, so while it may be on its astral travel, there is a continuous link to our living earthly physical body and it will therefore find its way back.
■　　The consecrated Circle we cast or the white light we draw down over ourselves prior to any meditation leading to astral travel or energy work, will further reinforce our protection and serve as our natural defence against any evil.

This applies, unless we purposefully choose to invite evil and malicious entities, practice substance abuse, have a serious character flaw or display any other unsavory characteristics, which would leave us open and vulnerable to attack. Such intentions are, under no circumstances, part of Craft practice in any shape or form!.

Methods of Otherworld Travel

Assuming that we are working toward the highest ideals of Spirit and the Divine, as we always should, and are psychically protected within our consecrated Circle surrounded by white light, we can transcend our earthly physical bodies through focused will, meditation and visualization or use Astral body, or Ethereal body to access the Otherworld and its Astral and Mental Realm. These are different words to describe the same experience. As mentioned, the Astral body is always connected to the earthly body via the Silver Cord, which is only severed upon death, when the Astral or Etheric body finally ascends to dwell on the Astral plane in Summerland, to 'one day', return in a new incarnation on Earth.

Through focused visualization and a familiar chosen cosmological map, be it the Kabbalistic Tree of Life; the OTz ChIIM or the Three Worlds of Norse Mythology or the Eastern Seven Planes of Existence, we leave the earthly realm, moving through ether, in vibrational tune with the coursing energy fields to reach our destination, normally via one of two methods:

The first, via Astral Projection, by perceiving the Astral Plane, at will, through visualization and meditation. The second method is by using the senses in conjunction with the Four Doorways of the Four Elements, again, through visualization in meditation. In this way we pass through the Four Worlds, as defined by, for example, the Kabbalstic Tree of Life with each reflecting and corresponding to the already discussed four realms.

We will access the Four Kabbalistic Worlds as manifest within each realm, so that each realm can be experienced via the four Elements with their corresponding physical senses; corresponding thus: Earth – Touch, Water – Taste, Fire – Sight; Physical and Spiritual, Air ~ Smell. This is often initiated via guided meditation, or, if you are fully proficient, via your powers of visualization and your own personal cosmological map read by your mind's eye.

Depending what you wish to experience on the Otherworld realms,

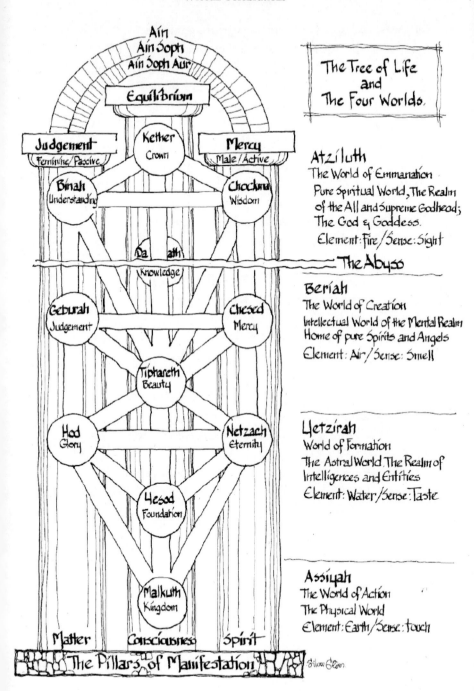

The Tree of Life
and
The Four Worlds.

Ain
Ain Soph
Ain Soph Aur

Equilibrium

Judgement
Feminine/Passive

Kether
Crown

Mercy
Male/Active

Atziluth
The World of Emmanation
Pure Spiritual World, The Realm
of the All and Supreme Godhead;
The God & Goddess.
Element: Fire / Sense: Sight

Binah
Understanding

Chockma
Wisdom

Da   ath
Knowledge

The Abyss

Geburah
Judgement

Chesed
Mercy

Beriah
The World of Creation
Intellectual World of the Mental Realm
Home of pure Spirits and Angels
Element: Air / Sense: Smell

Tiphareth
Beauty

Hod
Glory

Netzach
Eternity

Yetzirah
World of Formation
The Astral World, The Realm of
Intelligences and Entities
Element: Water / Sense: Taste

Yesod
Foundation

Malkuth
Kingdom

Assiyah
The World of Action
The Physical World
Element: Earth / Sense: touch

Matter   Consciousness   Spirit

The Pillars of Manifestation

you may wish to exit or enter using different elemental portals or gateways. An example, very briefly:

You leave via the Portal of Earth, the Physical World ruling the sense of touch, as you possibly feel a wind rush over the skin. This is the World of Assiah, the World of Action and the actual physical substance of the Universe.

You pass through the Portal of Water as you taste the crystal clear water of a rushing waterfall, as you pass through the sensuous realm of the Astral World with its many sub-planes, known as the World of Yetzirah, the World of Formation and the realm of intelligences and angels governing the stars and the planets. You may choose to dwell here or move on.

You pass through the Portal of Air and feel the heightened experience of Spiritual Insight as you enter the intellectual World of the Mental Realm. This is the realm of Briah, the World of Creation and home of pure Spirits and Higher Beings. We conduct formative work here, which is further manifest in the World of Yetzirah.

Although we are unlikely to ever experience this realm, we can visualize the Fourth Realm through the Portal of Fire, from a distance, through its multiple pure scents and its pure radiant endless light. This is the World of Atziluth, the Spiritual World and Archetypal World of Emanation and the realm of eternal primordial Nothingness. This is the realm of the Supreme Godhead, our God and Goddess.

Application in our Craft Life

How does this help us in our daily lives, our Craft practice and in gaining wisdom and enlightenment?

As the Unconscious informs us via dream symbolism about our inner self, the Otherworld informs us about our outer selves with its entities, guides and teachers advising us through intuition, meditation, 'sixth sense' and various ways about our state of our life, state of enlightenment, spiritual progress and performance within it. Considering that we use only a small fraction of our brain and can't explain what happens with the rest of our brain, we do, however, sense that we have faculties, latent abilities and potential that could serve to heighten our awareness, strengthen our bond with Nature, our God and Goddess and the Cosmos with its vast energies of which we are a part.

Through harnessing our mental faculties and focusing our mind we can access a realm of knowledge not found within our conscious and unconscious, {hence this realm is called the Otherworld}.
We have already understood that the power of mind is all encompassing and that the enactment of magick and mental transmutation is a product of will and control of all mental faculties.

Creation and Manifestation of Thought-forms

The Otherworld enables us to generate and manifest our own thought-forms, to be in tune with other thought-forms, to help us understand our real Self better,
It enables us to be in tune with other people and their energies, to influence other thought-forms for the better, to better balance our own inner energies, to forge a direct link with our deities and entities and to create and forge a better harmony with Nature.
Working in sympathy with the energies of the Otherworld, through our mind's eye, enables us to do this as we are, in many ways, a material manifestation of the substances of the Otherworld and therefore resonate in synchronicity with the same vibrations of the Otherworld. This is the essence of living in Equilibrium, in Harmony and in Tune with Nature of which the Universe and its Laws, like ourselves, are a part.
Working in sympathy with the Universal energies enables us to mentally transmute thought-forms into action in the physical realm. We visualize the thought-form being created from No-thing within Atziluth, the World of Emanation gaining a vague identity

and intellectual content within Briah, the World of Creation, through the forces of Wisdom and Understanding, the two Sephirot on the Tree of Life governing the World of Briah.

From here the thought-form gains material density and increased manifestation as it descends to the realms of Yetzirah, the World of Formation, also known as the Astral World, with its many planes, until it fully manifests within the Material world of Assiah, the Physical World of Action and tangible Earth, where it becomes reality.

The Otherworld as source of Information

The Astral and Mental Plane therefore harbor a wealth of concepts and, as yet, unmanifest dreams, wishes and ideas, which explains how we can possibly see the future, if we wish, by traveling on the Astral Plane.

It is also in this manner that we can develop and create a thought-form within the Astral or Mental Plane for others to receive. In the same manner, we can hold a 'dialogue;' with others on the Astral Plane. It is also via the Otherworld Planes that we can communicate with our God and Goddess and any entities we wish to communicate with, as we 'see', 'sense' and 'feel' their presence, even though they are the Supreme Godhead, residing within Kether on the Tree of Life, the Sephira of the Atziluthic World, and beyond.

Otherworld Energies and Auras

Through clairvoyance, we can recognize the Astral bodies of others within the Earthly realm of our daily life, by tuning into their energy fields or auras. We can recognize, through the shape of the aura and predominance of the colors within it, their state of health, their stage of enlightenment and establish if they are in equilibrium with themselves.

The Otherworld as Home of the Akashic Records

The Otherworld as discussed is also the abode of the Akashic Records. This is the region filled with three high speed vibrations of the past, present and future oscillating simultaneously, creating energy and it is visually the brightest light on the Astral plane. This intense light forms a focal point or the center, as it were, within the Astral Realm thereby guiding the traveler directly to the Akashic Record's Hall. The physical form of the Record's Hall appears different to each individual whether it be a giant library, a continuous movie screen where our past lives are scrolled off, walls of TV screens where you can tune into different 'channel's bearing different information or a series of live enacted plays with music staged on revolving platforms. They are all personal and Spirit; the Divine, will use the right 'medium' most accessible to you and your preferences, when you wish to access this information. Many of us wish to gain access to our Akashic records as we can gain information about our spiritual past lives, gain an insight into our karmic debts of our current life to see where we can improve and learn in our current life. In this way we can find out where we need to learn to grow spiritually.

The Otherworld, Past Lives and Re-incarnation

As we believe that we gain insight through lessons learnt and through being sensitive and aware, we also understand that this cannot happen in one life time alone. Wicca believes that upon death on Earth our physical body transmutes into other physical matter, but the Soul; the Self; our Identity enters into the Spirit realm or, as we call it, The Summerland, located on one of the planes of the Astral Realm. Myth as a metaphor says that this is within the Otherworld and within the realm of the God, where he presides over a transition phase whereby our life is assessed, before our Soul moves on to be reborn in the next incarnation. In effect, the God assesses our life's record to see how we have progressed, in order to define, in a very broad format, what we need to learn in the next incarnation. It is up to us how we further define and develop our own future life map.

Essentially, non-physical matter such as the Soul, or Self cannot be destroyed or transmuted allowing us to evolve in wisdom over many life times giving rise to the concept of Past Lives.

As mentioned, we can access our Akashic Records located on the Astral Realm with help from our teachers and guides to find out more about our Past Lives, our Karmic debts and possible future courses of our new life incarnation.

It must be remembered that none of this has been scientifically proven or otherwise, so it is subjective personal experience and still accepted as myth, belief and faith.

Lets investigate Past Lives further:
If we accept that our lives evolve through many incarnations in order to attain a fully integrated Self or Soul, then we accept that we retain and carry over material learnt from past incarnations forming the storehouse and basis of our thought-forms, symbols, talents, abilities, predispositions and the Souls identity in the next incarnation. Thus the individual identity grows.

The Summerland within the Otherworld is also the 'Transition Station' where our karmic debts, as recorded within our Akashic Records are resolved, so the new life can begin free of any unresolved issues, although some traditions believe that karmic lessons are carried through successive lives, until resolved. Personally, seeing that Wicca teaches that reincarnation is the process to insight and perfection, I can accept that unresolved karmic issues are processed with our Guides, Teachers and Gods' help in the Summerland, until we have learnt the appropriate lessons even if it takes many years or many hundreds of years before we reincarnate.

RITUAL

Previously we discussed the concept of the different Worlds. Now we will consider the method and ways in which we celebrate our connection to the God and Goddess, Entities, Angels, Guides, the Elements and Nature as a Whole.

The aim of Ritual is to achieve an altered state of mind, {very definitely not through substance abuse!}. This is entirely through our own will, control, the power of visualization and the generation of energy, in an entirely sober state whether done as a Solitary or within a Coven situation. The aim of ritual is to create a heightened state of awareness, a greater focus, a stronger bond between your inner Self, the Soul, the Higher Forces and the Divine.

In Wicca everything to do with Ritual aims to achieve this, whether it is the time of day the Sabbat or Esbat is held, the colors of our robes and altar cloths, all insignia, sigils, symbols, the smell of incense, the use of candles and light, the design and the types of tools, and the materials we use during the ritual, such as salt, water, incense and oils. Each symbol in the form of a tool, material or color represents the microcosm of the larger macrocosm or the Greater Whole. They all serve to heighten the senses, to sharpen and focus the mind on the forthcoming events to create and strengthen the bond between our deities, Nature and the All.

Myth and Symbolism

Myth often plays out life experiences or re-enacts sequences of life, metaphorically and symbolically, forming a direct link to the unconscious brain that recognizes the symbolism. In this way, members of a Coven or the solitary Witch enacting the myth form a personal relationship with the symbolism, thereby resulting in a clear understanding and insight, as all sections of the brain are used:

the unconscious as well as the conscious, as the Rite is performed in a waking conscious state. In this way, it can be said, the ritual serves to reconcile the two halves of the psyche. Through this reconciliation the individual forms a stronger bond with the greater cosmic energies, essential for any energy work to be done.

This is a key manner in which the ritual and its structure serve to bring about greater integration within the practitioner, as it relates to, and utilizes both the conscious and unconscious mind.

In Wicca we believe that we can only bring about successful and powerful energy work, as an integrated human being because only then, do we begin to really understand our full potential; the enactment and the practice of a well structured ritual greatly serves to bring this about.

Raymond Buckland, in his book *"Buckland's Complete Book of Witchcraft"*, Llewellyn Publications, USA, 2004 explains that there are two essential components to Ritual, namely, the Legomena and the Dromena. These terms derive from the Ancient Greek and refer to 'Things Said' {Legomena} and 'Things Done' {Dromena}. Together they form a 'Rite', or the formal Act of Religion with form implying a definite structure. In Wicca these are: The Casting of the Circle and its Consecration, The Calling of the Quarters, though in some traditions, this is only required under certain circumstances, Inviting of the God and Goddess, the Rite itself, Cakes and Wine, Thanking the Elementals/ Watchtowers/ Quarters and the God and Goddess for attending, Clearing the Circle/ Temple.

The structure of the Rite depends on whether it is for a Sabbat celebration or a working Esbat. I believe that Rites can also be used for deep meditation requiring energy work in which you may wish to commune with the God and Goddess. Such Rites can also be very successful teaching tools, for as mentioned above, they require all aspects of the brain to be used and as such help to directly focus the mind on a chosen subject.

Furthermore, in the case of a Coven meeting good successful ritual requires as much participation as possible of all members present. In the end, both Sabbats and Esbats are supposed to be joyous occasions which is why I have included such acts as the Coven Choral, - yes, the verses split up among many members can also be recited if no one feels like singing!, Call and Answer, Dance, Chants, as well as the use of a selection of musical instruments for improvised use.

The emphasis is on group activity to create a memorable and joyous occasion strengthening the bond between the individual members to engender a feeling of the Coven as a family. Group activity is essential for any successful group energy work, where the Coven is expected to work as one melded energy source.

Symbolism in Things Said and Done: Legomena and Dromena

Let us briefly look at some of the symbolism when conducting Ritual:
We cast our circle, symbolizing the Cosmos as the Universe on Earth, in a deosil direction, meaning 'sun wise'; that is from East to West. This is to symbolize that the performance of the Ritual is in harmony with nature, in sequence with nature's cycle and is taking place in the light and energy of the Sun and Moon.

Just after the High Priestess or the High Priest has announced that the Rite has begun, they can state that we:, *"Stand on the Threshold between the Worlds"*. This is seen on a number of levels: firstly, we wish to define the Circle space as separate and set it apart from our daily mundane lives as through conducting the Ritual, we should undergo an inner change as we work with energies and powers within our consecrated Circle. We are creating our own microcosm within the Circle, a sacred consecrated space in which we wish to conduct a divine and religious act working with energies and

powers within our consecrated Circle. We will then be calling on
the Watchers, or the Watchtowers, the major forces of the Universe
whose primary role is to guard and protect our Circle if we will
be conducting energy work requiring the invocation of different
entities. Then we could invite the Quarters; the Elementals,
Universe's Nature Spirits and the Rulers of the Four Elements, if we
wish and it is appropriate to the work we need to do as part of the
Rite. We can certainly invite the God and Goddess, if appropriate
and the nature of the work is important enough.

We should be calm, grounded and at peace as we experience a shift
in consciousness as we focus on divine powers present and generate
energies within ourselves bringing about a heightened awareness.
We can draw energy up into ourselves from the depths of the earth
or down into ourselves from the higher realms, or both. At this stage,
we are experiencing a transition away from the mundane world.
Through the Ritual acting as vehicle, its focus and energies and
our powers of visualization, we form a direct link of power with the
greater powers, which we should feel physically and very definitely
spiritually and mentally.

Our senses and faculties will be sharpened and heightened. Some of
us can then see and hear 'deeply and remotely'. Our sense of touch
and smell is exponentially stronger and more sensitive as in our
normal waking lives. Colors are brighter and more luminous, scale
distorts and sounds are so much clearer. In this state it is likely that
we will feel the presence of entities in different ways, if not in some
cases, even see them.

In this state, we are considered to be incorporated into a different
energy field. This is what is meant by "Standing between the
Worlds", our mundane world and the world of Energy – it very
definitely encapsulates that shift in consciousness that causes
all facets of the brain to work, harnessing energy via all faculties
to create a heightened state of awareness, which we need to
successfully practice the Craft side of Wicca.

THE CIRCLE

The Circle is in fact cast as two parts, the 'inner round', Circle itself and the outer protective bastion, with a gap in-between. This gap works like a transition area for magickal energy and thought-forms to pass from our sacred Circle via the material world into the Astral Plane. In doing this, energy leaves our magick Circle and the portals of the Elemental Rulers guarding the inner Circle, via the transition zone, or gap leaving via the Watchtowers guarding the portals of the outer Bastion, the Watchtowers' bastion forming the external boundary to the Otherworld and outer dimensions.

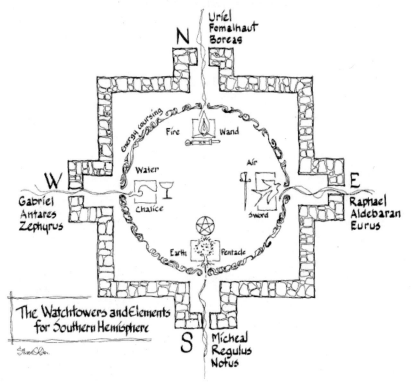

This outer 'Circle' is best visualized as a square resembling a fortress complete with ramparts, castellated walls and four guard towers at each compass point. Depending on tradition and/ or cultural background, the Watchers; those primal protective guardian forces of the Universe, can be visualized as the four Archangels of the Kabbalistic tradition, located at the compass points thus:

For the Northern Hemisphere:

Compass Direction	Archangel
North	Uriel
West	Gabriel
East	Raphael
South	Michael

For Southern Hemisphere, interchange the name for the North and South.

Visualizing a medieval scene, they would be facing outward in their protective role 'screening' all entities and energies arriving at the compass point entrances, allowing only those entry who have good intentions and whom we have invited/ invoked.

Some traditions are inspired by the ancient Mesopotamian myth of the Four Royal Stars, four of the brightest and most powerful stars on the firmament, as Watchers:

For the Northern Hemisphere:

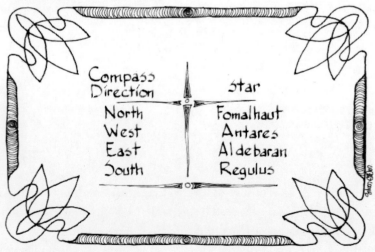

Compass Direction	Star
North	Fomalhaut
West	Antares
East	Aldebaran
South	Regulus

For Southern Hemisphere, interchange the name for the North and South
Visually the Four Royal Stars protect through Fire and Light, blazing away evil and unwanted entities.

An alternative, used in some traditions, is to invoke the Four Winds of Greco-Roman mythology, sweeping away any malicious intent, will or entity. They are:
For the Northern Hemisphere:

Compass Direction	Wind
North	Boreas
West	Zephyrus
East	Eurus
South	Notus

For Southern Hemisphere, interchange the name for the North and South.

Personally, I enjoy visualizing the Archangels assisted by the Royal Stars above them, standing guard at the Watchtowers of the fortress.

The Four Compass points represent the four classical Elements; the Quarters, on the inner Circle being Earth, Air, Fire and Water without which life on Earth would not be possible. Together they are all life giving and life sustaining. Fire is related to the direction of the Sun and the Sun itself, with its direct link to the Equator and the Tropics giving us the Seasons. Earth has a direct relationship to the North and South Pole, the Axis points of the Earth, as well as the Land, our habitat. Water relates to the Sea while Air relates to the wind, sky and Cosmos.

Symbolically, the colors of the Southern Hemisphere Quarter candles representing the Elemental Rulers are:
For Southern Hemisphere:

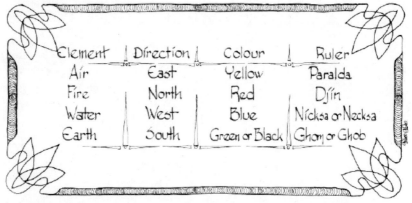

Element	Direction	Colour	Ruler
Air	East	Yellow	Paralda
Fire	North	Red	Djin
Water	West	Blue	Nicksa or Necksa
Earth	South	Green or Black	Ghom or Ghob

The above are the standard colors which vary in certain traditions.

In the Northern Hemisphere, the Quarters would be located on the Circle line thus:

Element	Direction	Colour	Ruler
Air	East	Yellow	Paralda
Earth	North	Black or Green	Ghom or Ghob
Water	West	Blue	Nicksa or Necksa
Fire	South	Red	Djin

The above standard colors vary depending on tradition.

The Fifth Element, Spirit also known as Ether, is not represented by a candle as such, but forms the apex above the Circle, below which most traditions locate the Altar. Some traditions choose to locate the Altar to the side of the Circle, close to the Northern or Eastern Quarter. By locating the Altar in the center of the Circle, it symbolically forms a direct link with the Spirit of the All, above and around us. Any energy work done within the Circle, is said to generate a 'cone of power' which is visualized as an upended ice cream cone over the Circle, its point over the center forming the direct link with Spirit. The ritual is therefore performed by the light and under the guidance of Spirit and the Divine.

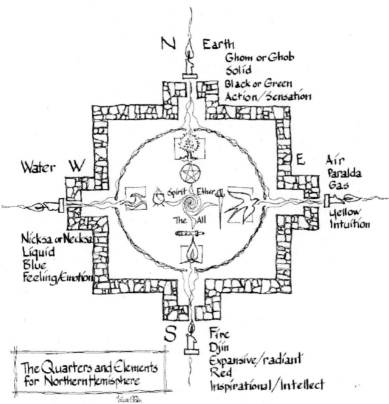

It is interesting to understand the full potential of inviting the Rulers of the Elements and the Elementals; the Nature Spirits governing the relevant Element to your Rites. All work we do is Nature based using the forces or energies of Nature, which includes the Universe and the Cosmos. The ebb and flow of life and energy is directly related to the forces of the Elements. To me, it is therefore important that the Rulers of the Elements or the Elementals themselves are invited when energy work is done, depending on the nature of the work itself. The Elementals are visualized in many different ways, eg: force fields, Faeries and variations of the Lords, Kings or Rulers of the respective Element itself. They act and feel more like an abstract force dwelling on the outer planes endowed with qualities controlling their particular Element while on the physical plane, they prefer to reside in areas where their particular Element prevails, eg: around creeks and springs, forests, mountain tops and rock outcrops.

The Rite of Invoking the Quarters, with its metaphor and symbolism serves to align us with these different psychological states, functions and qualities. Their energies help to heighten our perception and faculties as we interact with their forces on the higher planes. The interplay of,- together with our working and harnessing Elemental energy stimulates or neutralizes aspects of our personalities to help us achieve our intent in our work, whether that be formulating and transmitting a thought-form on the astral plane or accessing information about certain aspects of ourselves, or any other relevant energy work.

A direct link; an attunement and communion with the relevant Spirits of Nature ruling Earth, Water, Air and Fire is essential for meaningful, successful and profound energy work. In the end, our entire way of life and Pagan belief system is based on Nature and the energies of Earth, Fire, Air and Water with Spirit presiding as the archetypal Guide and Force. We would not exist without them.

The Rulers of the Elements and Elementals would be invited and would be facing the Rite with their energies and powers forming an integral part of all work. One or other elemental energy may be more prevalent, depending on the nature and intent of the work.

Furthermore, depending on the requirements of the work, we need to draw either Earth, Air, Fire and Water energies into ourselves to create a heightened sense of the element in order to use its power relevant to the work related to it.

Briefly, attributes and properties related to the Elements are:

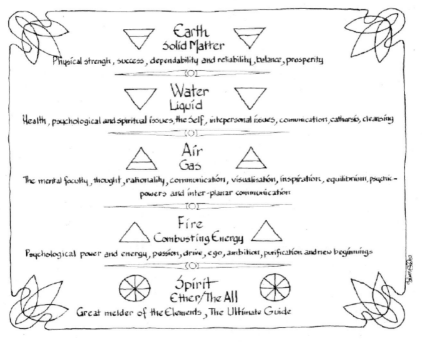

Spirit, the Fifth Element is always present at all times as the white light of protection we call upon at the beginning of all our Rites. Spirit, Ether, the Fifth Element is the Archetypal protector and guide.

The Circle itself is to be visualized as a three dimensional globe or sphere with a central axis and a horizon or equator. The Equator symbolizes the cast Circle as we scribe it in real life while the axis is the connection between the Worlds. Below the horizon; the Circle;

the Equator, is the Underworld to be visualized as being below your feet when standing inside the Circle. The Middleworld or the Physical and Material Realm in which we are conducting the Rite, is visualized as a narrow band, or sliver, above the horizon or Equator. The Otherworld comprises the dome or globe above the equator. The casting of the Circle should be visualized as creating this globe or sphere encompassing the Three Worlds; it is the creation of the microcosm of the macrocosm within which we *stand between the Worlds*

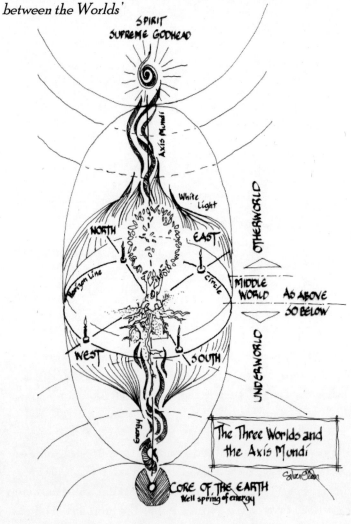

The Three Worlds and the Axis Mundi

The Central axis much like the Earth's axis, forms the connection between the Worlds. In conducting the Rite at the Altar we form the axis while drawing energy up from the wellspring of the Earths core and down form the Cosmos above. At the Altar we stand below the apex forming a conduit of energy between the worlds as we conduct the ritual. The highest point of the axis is Spirit, which pervades, infuses and is ever present in all worlds, all realms, all planes and within us as we conduct the ritual.

The central axis can also be visualized as energies drawn down and/or up via the Chakras, or personal power centers, which are then transmitted as a continuous flow of energy transmitted from person to person within the Circle forming an ever strengthening bond of growing power and ever increasing vibrations. This is what is described as the 'Cone of Power'. The Circle, visualized as a globe or sphere forms the envelope of light and container of positive energies acting as psychic protection from any potential evil intent or threat from outside.

Moreover, it is also seen as the envelope containing and retaining all positive energies generated during the ritual. It is the locus of the sacred and the light, presided over by the God and Goddess and Spirit as they are invoked and invited to the ritual. At the end of the ritual, all energies should be grounded with the essence of these energies having infused all who attended in the form of love, a positive state of mind, a feeling of elation and supreme happiness.

The Four Elements and Spirit are also represented in Wicca's symbol: the circumscribed Pentagram, with each point signifying one Element with Spirit being located at the top most centrally located point.

The Pentagram in Wicca, is always shown and worn, with one point upright, namely signifying Spirit and therefore enlightenment ruling over all other Elements, except when used by certain traditions for their Second Degree initiation where it is reversed.

This is the only time when
the Pentagram is reversed,
to symbolize the very steep
path we need to take and
come to terms with when
facing our Shadow side,
our dark side, our vices,
our negative side, our bad
habits and failures. The
Pentagram is reversed,
symbolizing how far we
digress from the guiding
light of Spirit, as the single
point is pointing down.
Once we have successfully

The Pentagram

completed our Second Degree and have cast light into our darkest
shadows through insight and knowledge and have found the way
to Spirit, the Pentagram is turned the right way up, with the 'Spirit
point' up. The Pentagram is circumscribed, i.e. the Star sits in a circle,
symbolizing the Whole, the Cosmos much like the Circle in which
we hold our Rituals. The Circle also symbolizes infinity, the never
ending, timeless, space without end, like the Universe of which we
are a part.

When we draw the invoking Pentagram of the Earth at the
consecration of the individual Rites we visualize the star as we
scribe it with our Athame or Wand starting at the apex of Spirit
drawing the left hand downward stroke to the 'Earth point', we are
symbolically drawing the light and energy of Spirit down to the
Earth, our microcosm and the locus of our life and Ritual. We further
scribe the line from the 'Earth point' to the right and to the 'Water
point', then across to the left and to the 'Air point', then down to the
right and to the 'Fire point', then back to the apex of Spirit. Thereby
we have named and addressed the Elements of life and the essence
of life they represent to infuse our Rite: the purifying properties of

Water, the breath of life of Air, the energy of Fire, the stability of the Earth. We have conducted the Rite in the light of Spirit and consecrated the action to the Divine.

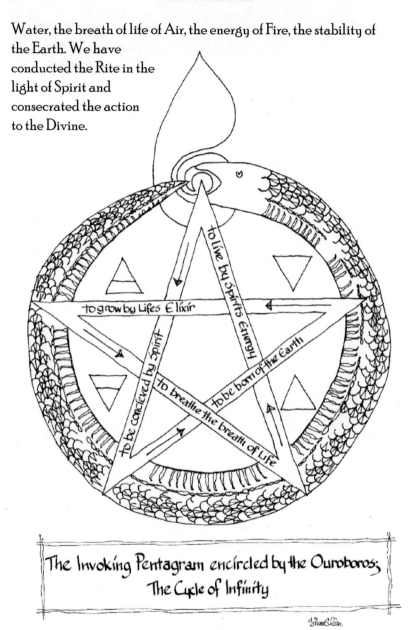

The Invoking Pentagram encircled by the Ouroboros; The Cycle of Infinity

The banishing Pentagram is scribed in reverse, whereby we are symbolically reversing the energy flow at the end of the Rite. We are consecrating the residual positive essence of the Rite, of love and joy to Spirit.

In some traditions the Quarter Rulers are invoked or invited by scribing the invoking Pentagram of the Air, Water, Earth and Fire above each candle set at the relevant Quarter. The relevant invoking Pentagram is scribed above the relevant tool presented to each Element at the appropriate Quarter and Invoking stage of the Rite. These tools are:

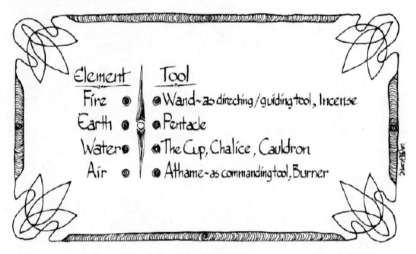

Element	Tool
Fire	Wand – as directing/guiding tool, Incense
Earth	Pentacle
Water	The Cup, Chalice, Cauldron
Air	Athame – as commanding tool, Burner

It must be noted that the invoking Pentagram of Air, Water and Fire are scribed starting at the opposite point to the Element being invoked. The symbolism of tracing the line of the pentagram from the opposing Element serves to highlight the gender polarity without which no 'reaction' can take place.

The exception is Spirit, transcending gender definition, as the vehicle which melds the Elements together. The invoking Pentagram of the Earth is the most often used, as explained, symbolically displaying how we draw the Light of Spirit to our Rite, held in our 'home', the Earth.

In many traditions the Sword and the Athame, being commanding tools, are attributed to the Element of Air, the masculine Element. They would be consecrated by the invoking Pentagram of Air. Similarly, the Cauldron and the Chalice are tools attributed to the

Element of Water, the feminine Element. The Wand, the guiding and directional tool is often attributed to the Element of Fire, a masculine Element, while the Pentacle symbolizes the Earth, the feminine Element attributed to the Goddess.

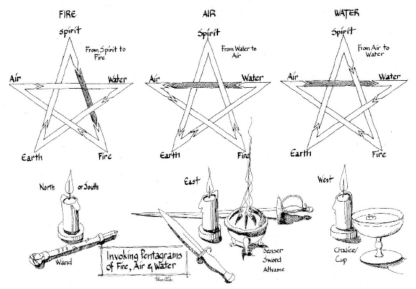

We consecrate the Four Elements in the name of the God and Goddess in the form of two sets of Divine Unions symbolizing the polarity found in Nature, thus: Earth and Water are consecrated to the Goddess, as both complement each other to be fertile. Fire and Air are consecrated to the God, as complementary in terms of action and dynamism. Fire and Air as Light and Oxygen, properties of the God, complement Earth and Water, realms of the Goddess, ensuring life. In this way all four Elements together, form the whole of the Microcosm of life on Earth and the God and Goddess are manifest as the binary team.

When consecrating the Circle after it has been first 'scribed' with the Athame or wand, we walk along its edge in a deosil manner and sprinkle it with consecrated Water, mixed with salt, both having been blessed prior to their mixing. The Water is used for its life giving properties and the Salt has two meanings; firstly as semen or seed as life giving, the other is Salt as the purifying ingredient that drives out impurities from the Water so that we are consecrating the Circle with pure, uncontaminated, positively charged Water. Water, as we see in our oceans and rivers is easily polluted. Next, we walk along the edge of the Circle carrying the censer with the burning incense. This symbolizes Fire and Air and the smoke serves to purify the air of all negativity.

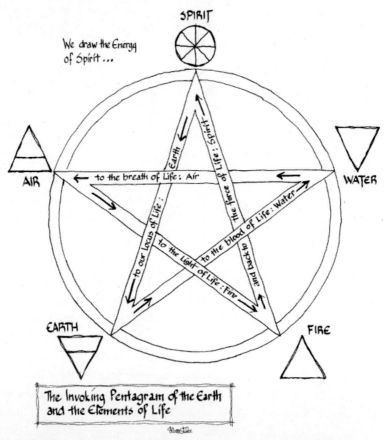

The Invoking Pentagram of the Earth and the Elements of Life

After having cleansed with Fire and Air we then consecrate the Circle with Light by walking the perimeter carrying a candle lighting each Quarter candle in turn, to invoke positive energies and infuse our work with light, insight and positivism. The Light also serves to banish any negative energies that may hang around the

Circle site.

We have now consecrated the Circle with Earth {Salt} and purified Water, Ether {Air and Fire} and Light {Sun/Fire}. The final step in Circle casting is to walk the Circle perimeter again 're-scribing' the Circle with our Athame or Wand to seal and strengthen it in definition and protection.

Finally, at Sabbats and Esbats we anoint ourselves, as a Solitary Witch, or anoint each other in a Coven situation. Normally the opposite sex, wherever possible, anointing the opposite sex, again to symbolize the polarity found in nature. The symbolism of the anointing is to show that we identify with the God and Goddess and feel at one with them while conducting the ritual.

 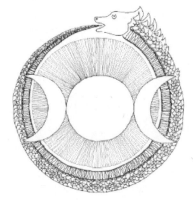

THE FOUR ELEMENTS AND SPIRIT

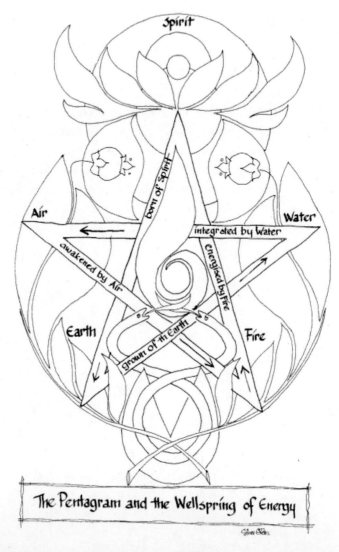

The Pentagram and the Wellspring of Energy

All of Creation is infused and animated by the forces and attributes of the Four Elements and Spirit, as they are symbolized by the Pentagram; Earth, Air, Water, Fire and Spirit, being the top most point of the Star. All that is manifest around us emanates from the Source of All Things and all bears the Divine Spark of that which created it. All is therefore formed as a concept and manifests through the realms of creation until it reaches The Physical Plane of the Middleworld, the realm of dense matter, where it takes material form and shape.

We, as human beings are an integral part of the All, having been created by the Source of All Things; we are also manifest through the Four Elements as they sustain us in life, through the air we breath, the water that's integral to our bodies functioning, the light we need to live and see by and the Earth that supports us in life and life style.

It is through the Four Elements and Spirit that we experience life on the Physical Plane of Earth.

We, as human beings are also subject to the energies and forces of the Four Elements and *The All* in that the energies of Fire support the functioning of our nervous system; Water regulates our emotional system; Air supports our mental faculties and Earth regulates our Soul's stability. Furthermore, the Four Elements allow us to sense and perceive, in that Fire corresponds to our sense of vision; our sense of smell and taste is manifest through Air; our emotions, sense of hearing and the cumulative resources of all senses are manifest through the Element of Water; while our sense of touch is governed by Earth. The stabilizing properties of Earth also form the catalyst through which all our perceptions created via the senses, are understood. Earth is also the element through which we ground ourselves after having done energy work, using all our perceptive senses after opening up our energy centers and using them as conduits. The Four Elements and Spirit thus allow us to function, perceive, and work in harmony with its energies and powers within the Physical Realm of the Middleworld. It is also via the powers and the Four Elements that we can align ourselves to raise power to create thought-forms on the higher realms.

It is therefore not surprising to see that the complementary Elements such as Fire and Air, Realm of the God are responsible for our mental and intellectual faculties. They both harmonize in governing our ability to visualize and form thought-forms and to communicate them. Fire gives us the energy to transmit the thought form.

Water and Earth, the Realm of the Goddess, forms the other complementary pair of Elements. Water governs our emotions, which are fluid in nature, while the stability of Earth serves to stabilize us emotionally and mentally. The stability of Earth also helps us to grow in wisdom by allowing us to ground and center in order to absorb and take in the essence of what we are trying to learn.

The Fifth Element of Spirit presides over all manifestations and provides the framework for all energy work and magick to take place within Light and Positive Energy and protection of the Divine.

Elemental energy also exists in our psychological realm and is a key to self-realization, growth and psychological development. Carl Gustav Jung believed that people can be defined as four different character types by displaying four unique different types of characteristics, of which one or more predominate, based on the quality of the Elements. It is the Elemental nature that dictate personality and the character of the person. It is through the balance or the imbalance of attributes that we become stable or instable. They are:

■ The Phlegmatic Person in whose character the Element of Earth prevails. This persons perception of the world would be largely informed by sensation, through the physical senses.

■ The Melancholic Person in whom the qualities of the Element of Water prevail in that their perception of the world is governed through feeling, in assessing what's good and bad.

■ The Sanguine Person's character is largely defined by the qualities of Air in that their perception of the world is informed through rational, logical and analytical thinking. This person is largely grounded in the present.

■ The Choleric Person is largely ruled by the Element of Fire, relying to a large extent on their intuition to inform themselves about the world around them. The choleric gains insight via the imagination and intuition and sees life more in terms of future events, likely future scenarios and potential happenings taking place.

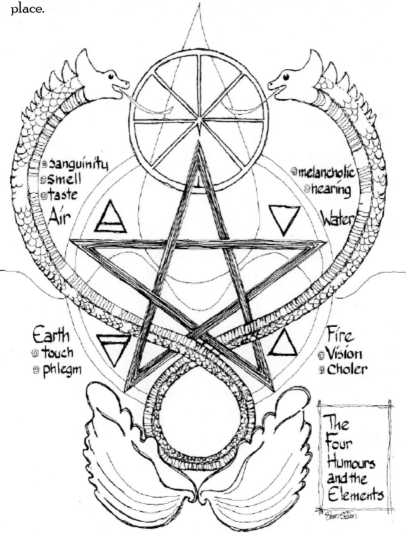

Sanguinity
Smell
taste
Air

melancholic
hearing
Water

Earth
touch
phlegm

Fire
Vision
Choler

The
Four
Humours
and the
Elements

The above categorization of personality types is based of the ancient Greek concept of the *Four Humours* and their study of how human character can be defined in terms of the qualities of the Four Elements.

The interplay of the Elemental energies help us integrate. The vehicle and synthesis of different ratios of the Elements assist us in accessing realms where we gain insight into ourselves such as the Underworld, the realm of our Shadow-side, in order to bring light to the darkness there. It is through the Element of Air and Fire that we bring intellectual insight to cast light into the dark, to better integrate our dark side with our light side. It is through the integration of the Element of Water and Earth that we, as human beings integrate and become stable by what we learnt from our Underworld Shadow-side. It is through the mental correspondence of the Element of Air that we can access the Akashic Records on the Astral Plane to gain insight into our situation and state of being on the higher levels. It is also the intellectual energies of Air that assists us in integrating insights we have gained there.

As seekers if insight, integration, experience and knowledge we use the essence, vehicles and attributes of the Elements, every day, in all that we do by gleaning, synthesizing and applying knowledge and ability gained. It is also via the attributes of the Elements and the energies of the different Worlds and their realms that we practice on different levels, at different frequencies and different vibrational rates.

We are therefore definitely part of and subject to all the forces and Energies that affect the Cosmos and the Greater Whole or The All. This connection is formed via the Divine Spark we all carry within us. It is the properties of the Divine Spark as created by the Divine Source, that give us the latent potential to develop and evolve the required higher consciousness and perceptive powers to tune into the All and enact acts of magick.

By harnessing these latent powers and faculties within us we grow in the ability to generate acts of creation, such as thought-form transference, by mental visualization and stimuli, which in turn set vibrations in motion, causing actions and reactions on different levels to animate and activate entities and the divine on different planes. It is through our connectedness with Nature encompassing the Four Elements and Spirit through which all life manifests, that we can cause these changes to happen and activate on the Astral plane, setting in motion the corresponding responses in other realms so that forces can manifest in the material physical realm of the Earth.

We can do this, once practiced at the art, because we are an integral part of and an extension of the very forces and energies that pervade the All. We are a material manifestation of the same cause and effect forces that brought about the Divine Source of all Things of which we bear the Spark, our eternal connection to the All.

NOTES ON SOUTHERN HEMISPHERE PRACTICE

I live and work in the Southern Hemisphere; in Australia, therefore some key aspects of the Ritual and the celebration of the Sabbats and Esbats are "reversed":
Winter in the Southern Hemisphere corresponds to the Northern Hemisphere Summer
The dates of the key Sabbats shift by 6 months

Other points to be mindful are:
Circle Casting
The Sun and Moon rise in the East but stand and course to the north in the Southern Hemisphere meaning that we cast our circle from right to left, which is 'sun wise' or deosil, in the Southern Hemisphere, although this may appear widdershins to the Northern Hemisphere practitioner. It is, however, deosil, i.e. meaning sun wise, as seen within the Southern Hemisphere context.

Quarter Compass Points
The Quarters as set out on the Circle, in the Southern Hemisphere, are thus:
North: Fire {Equator/ Sun's arc within the sky}
South: Earth {South Pole}
West: Water
East: Air

I locate the Altar in the center of the Circle, below the apex of Spirit above and face East, symbolic of new and growing energies, welcoming the rising Moon, the rising

Sun, and a new born day or night, thereby inviting the young and waxing energies of the day or night.

The above is evident in the writing that follows.

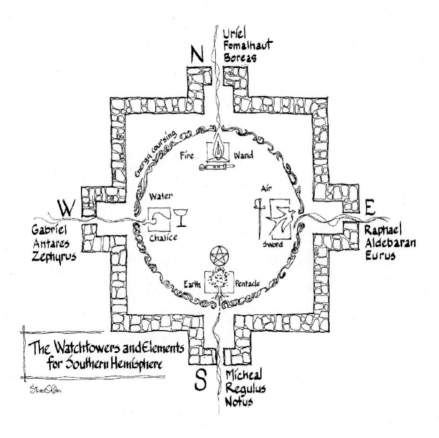

The Sabbats

The Sabbat Rituals

The actions in this section are common to each of the Sabbats.
They are referred to in all Sabbat celebrations
as being part of their Rituals
They are:

Preparation
Opening the Rite
Casting the Circle
Calling of the Quarters and Inviting the Deities
Cakes and Wine
Banishing of the Circle and Closing the Rite

Preparation

Define area of the Ritual
Mark out the Circle on the floor/ ground

Purification of the Circle Area
Sweep designated Circle area with besom/ ritual broom

Purification of the self
Bath/wash, dress, focus, meditate, practice deep breathing

Locate candle of appropriate color at Four Quarter points:

For the Southern Hemisphere:
East – yellow / Air – Elemental Ruler: Paralda
South – green / Earth - Elemental Ruler Ghom/ Ghob
West – blue / Water - Elemental Ruler: Niksa/ Neksa
North – red / Fire - Elemental Ruler: Djin

For the Northern Hemisphere:
East – yellow / Air – Elemental Ruler: Paralda
North – green / Earth - Elemental Ruler Ghom/ Ghob
West – blue / Water - Elemental Ruler: Niksa/ Neksa
South – red / Fire - Elemental Ruler: Djin

Use your own address or that used by your Coven/ Grove for the God and
Goddess, e.g: Lord and Lady
Use names of your choosing for the God and Goddess or the names used by
your Coven/ Grove
e.g: "Cernunnos and Aradia, daughter of Diana and Apollo"
Decide on an address for the Quarters, e.g: Rulers or Kings

Opening the Rite

The person designated as the Censerer lights the Altar candles for the God and
Goddess as well as the charcoal in the censer but not the Quarter candles.

80

He/ she leaves and joins the rest of the Coven waiting in the south-eastern area
outside of the Circle.
The High Priest {HP} and High Priestess {HPS} and the Master/ Maestro of
Ceremonies {MOC}*, or related, if your Coven/ Grove has such a structure,
enter the Circle from the South- Eastern side of the Eastern quarter candle.
*Note: although the Title says Master of Ceremonies, specific gender is
irrelevant!. HP, HPS and MOC stand before the Altar located at the center of
the Circle and face East. With their eyes closed they centre and channel energy
via the Chakras into hands and feet and focus on the event to follow.
The MOC sounds the Gong/ Chimes or Bell three times.
MOC, HP and HPS say in unison:

'This Rite has begun'

Casting the Circle

Depending on time of year, the HP or HPS scribes the Circle:
Light half of year: the HPS,
Dark half of year: HP
HP or HPS stands at the Altar, facing East and presents tool; Athame or Wand,
by raising it on the open flat palms of both hands to eye level or higher
HP or HPS moves deosil, or sunwise, to the Eastern Quarter taking tool in both
hands. He/she draws energy into themselves and the tool; from the centre of
the Earth via the soles of their feet and from the Cosmos through the crown
Chakra. He/she channels the energy into the tool and visualizes a blue-white
flame issuing from its tip, as he/ she points it at the marked out Circle, starting.
Slowly, he/ she starts in the East, walking deosil around the Circle, scribing the
Circle of white light onto the ground.
Note on Southern Hemisphere:
Deosil, meaning Sun Wise, is in the Southern Hemisphere from East, North,
West, South, back to East.
This needs to be reversed for Northern Hemisphere practice.

HP/ HPS says while walking:
I/ we cast this Circle in the Light of the Goddess and God
For it is our will
Your wish to fulfil
In the spirit of the Light
Honest, good and bright
Here may You manifest and bless your kin

HP or HPS move back to the Altar and replace their Athame/ Wand
The MOC sounds the gong/ chimes/ bell three times
The HP and HPS stand before the Altar facing East, he is on her right hand side
Coven still waits outside of the south-east quadrant
HP presents the chalice of water by lifting it to eye level and placing it onto the larger pentacle.
HP holds the Athame or Wand in clasped hands, as if in prayer gesture, with its tip over the water slowly lowering it to just over the water.

HP says:

As Neksa over Water reigns
Make it free from sullied stains
Cast out all that is impure
To bless our Circle sure

MOC strikes the gong once

HP says:

In the names of ... *{Fill in your own Deity names here}*

HP lays down his Athame/ Wand. He presents the bowl of salt and scrapes a little salt onto the smaller pentacle.
Again, using clasped hands similar to the prayer gesture, the HP points the tip of his Athame/ Wand over the salt

HP says:

Blessings be upon this Salt
Let all discord halt
As water it purifies
And divinely it sanctifies

MOC strikes the gong once

HP says:

In the names of ...
{Fill in your own Deity names here}

HP scrapes a little of the blessed salt from the pentacle into the water.
HP lifts the chalice of salted water, swirls it deosil three times and briefly raises it high over the Altar before walking deosil; starting and ending in the East around the Circle edge sprinkling blessed and consecrated water with an aspergillum or with the finger tips.
As he walks he says:

Water and Salt, here combine

Purified, blessed and divine
Water and Earth, Elements of Birth
May it protect our Circle cast
All discord away to blast

HP replaces the chalice on the Altar.

HPS presents tool; Athame or Wand. Then she presents the senser. She holds
the Wand/ Athame in clasped hands with its tip pointing over the burning
charcoal.

HPS says:

Fire, Elemental Ruler Djin
May our divine desire win
May blessings be upon this sacred flame
Free of discordant will and claim

MOC strikes the gong once

HPS says:

In the names of …
{Fill in your own Deity names here}

HPS presents the incense. She then places it onto the smaller pentacle. HPS
holds her Wand/ Athame in clasped hands with point down over the incense

HPS says:

Blessings be upon this incense sweet
Pure, divine, complete
Let Spirit's smoke inspire
May we hearken Your desire

MOC strikes the gong once

HPS says:

In the names of …
{Fill in your own Deity names here}

HPS lays down the Wand/ Athame and puts a small amount of the incense
onto the burning charcoal.
HPS lifts the burner high over the Altar and begins walking in a deosil direction,
starting and ending in the east, carrying the censer with the burning charcoal

and incense along the scribed Circle edge visualizing ether strengthening the protective barrier of the Circle edge.
As she walks, she says:

Air and Fire
Elements by Souls' require
Flight of thought and Souls' compassion
Directed in our Lord and Ladies' fashion
May they purify our Circle cone
From all discord prone

Upon returning to the East, the HPS replaces the censer on the Altar.

LIGHT

After having completed the initial scribing of the Circle, it is cleansed by consecrated water and further purified by ether symbolized by the smoking censer. It now needs to be illuminated by sacred light to raise the enclosed dome of pure white light. Depending on the waning or waxing time of the year, either the HP or the HPS carries the Light around the Circle; in other words, the person who will not be finally consecrating the Circle carries the Candle around the Circle periphery. They do this in silence, also lighting the Quarter candles as they go, visualizing how the light infuses the Ether.

CONSECRATING THE CIRCLE

Depending on whether it is the waning or the waxing or; the light or dark half of the year, the HP or the HPS repeats the first step by walking the scribed Circle edge again with his/ her Athame or Wand visualizing how the blue white light emanating from the tools' tip seals and reinforces the Circle edge. Again, he/ she starts and ends in the East walking deosil holding the tool with both hands directing the light beam at the scribed Circle on the ground.
He/ she does this in silence visualizing how the glowing Circle edge and the blue-white light pouring from the tool tip rises up to envelope the Circle space in a glowing iridescent dome of luminance reflecting light back into the Circle space.
HP or HPS returns to the Altar, replaces tool.

MOC strikes the gong once
MOC, HP, HPS stand at the altar facing East and say in Unison:
Round and round this Circle is bound
In Cosmic light on earthly ground
May no discord enter
Our Circle center
For this is our will

And so mote it be!

HP drops some of the already consecrated salt into the anointing oil and stirs with finger
He anoints the HPS with Celtic Cross; an equal armed cross set within a circle, on forehead
As he does so, he says:

In the name of the God and Goddess, I do thee anoint:
{Recite relevant Craft Name here}
As per Divine direction, They do thee appoint
And They bid thee enter
This sacred Circle centre

They salute {embrace and kiss}
HPS anoints the HP in same manner

She says:

In the name of the God and Goddess, I do thee anoint:
{Use relevant Craft Name here}
As per Divine direction, They do thee appoint
And They bid thee enter
This sacred Circle centre

HP or HPS anoint the MOC depending of whether the MOC is male or female

HP and HPS move to the East. One person carries the anointing oil while the other carries their Wand/ Athame: Consistent with the time of the year, the person who cast the Circle now scribes a doorway using his/ her Wand/ Athame starting at ground level scribing or cutting a doorway arch into the white light dome in a widdershins motion, ending at ground level on the other side. They visualize an entrance cut allowing the coven/ grove members to enter one by one by stepping over the threshold. As they enter, each member is anointed:

Males by the HPS

Females by the HP

HP or HPS says:

In the name of the God and Goddess, I do thee anoint:
{Use relevant Craft Names here}
As per Divine direction, They do thee appoint
And They bid thee enter
This sacred Circle centre

The Coveners stand about the Altar, as far as possible alternating male and female.

After the last one has been admitted either the HP or HPS re-scribes the doorway in a deosil direction, with his/ her Wand or Athame, starting at ground level, tracing the archway and ending again at ground level. While doing so, he/ she visualizes how white light fills the space and the glowing light dome is reinstated again. For good measure, the HP or HPS sprinkles a little of the oil over the closed doorway threshold, while the other draws the invoking Pentagram of the Earth above it, to fully seal it.

HP and HPS return to the Altar and replace the tools and the oil.
The MOC rings the chimes/ gong/ bell three times

HPS says:

In peace and love may ye gather here
Under Lunar/ Solar light, so clear
We bid ye hail and welcome!

MOC rings the smallest chime three times:
All:
Hail and Welcome

HP/ HPS returns to the Altar, facing East
HP/ HPS says:
{Traditional}
This is a time that is not a time
In a place that is not a place
On a day that is not a day
We stand at the threshold between the Worlds
As the Veil of Mystery unfurls

All in unison:
May the Old Ones protect us
Knowing our present, future, history
As we have vowed to hold true to the Craft
and the Old Ways
'Til the end of our Earth days
Now and forever aft

MOC rings the gong three times

MOC:
Let now the Quarters be saluted and the Gods invited
Give Thanks and celebrate them for love requited

Calling the Quarters

East:

HP and HPS each light a taper candle on the God and Goddess candle on the
Altar; the HP lights his on the Goddess candle while the HPS lights hers on the
God candle. They both move deosil around the Altar across to the East.
MOC strikes the Gong once
HPS, or designated Female Covener lights the East candle with the lit taper
candle

HPS or Female Covener says:
Here do we bring light to Air
Living iridescence fair
Air to breathe, life and light
Blessings on our Sabbat Rite

All face East in the Circle while saying:
Here do we bring light to the East
May it illuminate our Sabbat feast

North:

{in the Southern Hemisphere/ South in the Northern Hemisphere}
They move to the North
MOC strikes the gong once
HPS, or designated Female Covener lights the North candle

HPS or Female Covener says:
Here do we bring light to Fire
To fuel our drive, desire
Warmth and energy bright
Enliven our Sabbat night

All face North while saying:
Here do we bring light to the North

May its energy pour forth

West:
HP and HPS move to the West
MOC strikes the gong once
HP, or designated Male Covener lights the West candle

HP or designated Male Covener says:
Here do we bring light to Water
Venue of this Western Quarter
Water wash our Circle clean
Of all impurities unseen

All face West and say:
Here we bring light to the West
Brighten up our spiritual Quest

South
{in the Southern Hemisphere/ would be North in the Northern Hemisphere}
HP and HPS move to the South
MOC strikes the gong once
The HP or designated Male Covener lights the South candle

HP or Male Covener says:
Here do we bring light to Earth
Venue of our current birth
Earth for strength and power
At our Sabbat hour

All face South and say:
Here do we bring light to the South
May wise words stream from our mouth

Blessing the Quarters

East:
MOC strikes the chimes three times
A female Covener closest to the East turns outwards and moves to stand facing

the East candle
With her Athame/ Wand raised she draws the invoking Pentagram of the Air
above the already lit flame
Rest of the Coven face East and copy the movements made

She says:

Hail to the Element of Air
Ruler of the East
We bid Ye Welcome
And ask Ye to guard our Circle square

She kisses the tip of her Athame/ Wand and returns to the Circle

North:

{in the Southern Hemisphere but would be South in the Northern Hemisphere}
MOC strikes the chimes three times
A female Covener closest to the North, turns to face the already lit North
candle
With Athame/ Wand raised she draws the invoking Pentagram of the Fire.
Rest of the Coven face North and copy the movements made

She says:

Hail to the Element of Fire
Ruler of the North
We bid Ye Welcome
And ask Ye to guard our Circle's desire

She kisses the tip of her Athame/ Wand and returns to the Circle

West:

MOC strikes the chimes three times
A Male Covener closest to the West, turns to face the already lit West candle
With Athame raised he draws the invoking Pentagram of the Water.
Rest of the Coven face West and copy the movements made

He says:

Hail to the Element of Water
Ruler of the West
We bid Ye Welcome
And ask Ye to guard our Circle quest

He kisses the tip of his Athame/ Wand and returns to the circle

South:

{in the Southern Hemisphere but North in the Northern Hemisphere}
MOC strikes the chimes three times
A Male Covener closest to the South, turns to face the already lit South candle
With Athame/ Wand raised he draws the invoking Pentagram of the Earth.
Rest of the Coven face South and copy the movements made

He says:

Hail to the Element of Earth
Ruler of the South
We bid ye Welcome
And ask ye to guard our Circle girth

He kisses the tip of his Athame/ Wand and returns to the Circle

MOC strikes the gong once
HP stands at the Altar, facing East, draws the invoking Pentagram of the Earth
with his Athame above it

HP says:

Hail and Welcome to our Four Quarters
Elementals, Spirits, sons and daughters
We bid the Lord and Lady Welcome
In harmony, love and peace in sum

All:

We bid Ye all to witness here our Rite
This sacred Sabbat night

HP and HPS lay Athames/ Wands on Altar and raise their arms in salute

They say in unison:

Enliven and empower this event
By inspiration Spirit sent
We bid Ye enter our Circle task
Shield us from malice, this we ask

MOC strikes the gong once:
All:
Hail and Merry meet!

MOC strikes the gong once:
All:
Hail and Welcome!

The MOC rings the chimes three times.
The HPS says:
Now we're gathered here, the Circle is cast
With intentions clear, like centuries past
Let none leave sans good reason
As Spirits will aggrieve, spoiling season
Let us wait till the Circle is cleared
Energies grounded, Deities revered
And so mote it be!

All:
So mote it be!

The Sabbat Ritual appropriate to the date continues on from here.

The Cakes and Wine Rite and the Closing Circle Rite takes place after the appropriate Sabbat Ritual

Cakes and Wine/
Cakes and Juice/ Cakes and Ale/ Cakes and Mead
Soft drink is entirely appropriate here, should alcohol be an issue

All rise after the final Sabbat Rite, standing around the Circle alternating Male and Female as far as possible, facing inwards.

The Covener designated to keep the Altar Wine or Soft drink goblet filled, fills it
MOC sounds the gong three times to raise the Toast.
MOC presents the filled goblet with both hands, facing East and then raises it high above the Altar

MOC says:
Its time to give Thanks for the sustenance of body and mind
To our Lord and Lady with thoughts so dear and kind
May beauty and love abound
Within this Circle round

HP says:
May we be aware
About all that we share
And to the Gods we owe
For what we reap is what we sow

The HPS summons two Coveners, one male and one female
They step to the Altar and face one another.
The male takes the goblet in both hands, holding it in front of him, he kneels on one knee.
The female takes her Athame/ Wand and holds it with both palms, point down with its tip over the wine.

She says:
In like fashion
Our Lord and Lady join in passion
In happiness and love
For bounty, peace around, above

Male Covener says:
Let beauty and bounty thrive across the land
Wrought by Sacred spark and hand

Female Covener replaces her Athame/ Wand on the Altar and takes the goblet, the Male Covener rises and draws the Pentagram of Earth with his Athame/ Wand in the air above the goblet
Female Covener passes goblet for him to drink. He first pours a little wine onto the ground, if the Sabbat is held outside in the open or into the libation dish

before having a sip himself. He passes the goblet to the Female Covener who has a sip before she passes it on to make its round of the entire Circle. Upon return, the HP, HPS and MOC drink last.

MOC sounds the gong once
Female Covener takes up the plate of cakes and kneels on one knee.
Male Covener holds the point of his Athame/ Wand over them

He says:

The Lord and Lady wish us to share of their bounty
Throughout the land and county
So let us enjoy as we think
About our divine link
How they guide us on our way
Each minute, hour, day

Male Covener replaces the Athame/ Wand on the Altar and takes the plate of cakes from the female Covener.
She draws the Pentagram of the Earth with Athame or Wand above the cakes

saying:

Lets give thanks and share
And spare a thought and care
For the Gods we love
And their blessings from above

All:

So mote it be!

Female Covener replaces her Athame/ Wand on the Altar and offers the cakes to the Male Covener
He takes a cake, breaks a piece off and crumbles it in his fingers scattering the crumbs over the ground, if the Rite is held outside in the open. If not, he places the piece on the libation dish before eating the other piece himself. He then offers the plate to the Female who takes and eats before she passes the plate on to the Circle where it makes its rounds before arriving back at the Altar where the HP, HPS and the MOC eat last.

The MOC strikes the gong once

The HPS says:

May Their blessings here abound

Within this Circle round
So mote it be!
All:
So mote it be!

HPS motions all to sit
All sit, individual goblets are filled and the repast is enjoyed with any other
foods stored under the Altar being brought out to be enjoyed. It is a good time
for relaxation, talk and discussion. Some may enjoy playing instruments and
singing.

The Closing Rite

The fare-welling of the Quarters is done in a widdershins manner, meaning
anti-sunwise.
In the Southern Hemisphere this is from South to West, to North, to East and
back to South.
In the Northern Hemisphere this is from the North to West, to South to East
and back to North.
In the same manner, each Quarter is fare-welled by using the banishing
Pentagram of that Quarter/ Element.

MOC, HP and HPS stand at the Altar facing the East.
MOC sounds the Gong three times.
MOC:

As we did merry meet
we shall merry part
in love replete,
until our next meet start

HP and HPS present tool; Athame or Wand, raising it on open palms of both
hands to eye level or higher

SOUTH
{This would be North in the Northern Hemisphere}
HP moves to the Southern Quarter, faces South with Athame or Wand in his
hand
HPS stands to his right
MOC sounds the chimes once.
He draws the banishing Pentagram of the Earth above the black/ green candle.
He says:

Ruler of the South and Earth
Thank you for joining our Rite
This Sabbat night
We bid ye Hail and Farewell
Ave atque vale!

All:
Hail and Farewell!

All Coveners face South and copy the movements made by the HP
The Covener detailed by the HPS stands near the front to snuff out the South
candle in turn

WEST

The HP moves widdershins from the South to the West, followed by the HPS
He scribes the banishing Pentagram of Water in the air above the blue candle.
The MOC sounds the chime once

He says:
Ruler of the West and Water
Thank you for joining our Rite
This Sabbat night
We bid ye Hail and Farewell
Ave atque vale!

All Coveners face West and copy the movements made by the HP
All:
Hail and Farewell!

The person detailed by the HPS snuffs out the Western Quarter candle.

NORTH

{This would be South in the Northern Hemisphere}
The HP and HPS move to the North and the coven turns to face north.
The HPS steps forward and scribes the banishing Pentagram of Fire above the
Red candle
MOC sounds the chimes once
HPS says:
Ruler of the North and Fire

Thank you for joining our Rite
This Sabbat night
We bid ye Hail and Farewell
Ave atque vale!

The Coven copies the movements made by the HPS
All:
Hail and Farewell!

In recognition of the life Cycle of the Sun God, a central theme of the Sabbats, the Northern candle remains lit and is only extinguished once the God and Goddess and Altar candles are extinguished.

EAST
HP and HPS move widdershins to arrive at the Eastern Quarter.
The HPS steps forward and draws the banishing Pentagram above the yellow candle.
The MOC sounds the chimes once
She says
Ruler of the East and Air
Thank you for joining our Rite
This Sabbat night
We bid ye Hail and Farewell
Ave atque vale!

Coven moves to face East and copies the movements made by the HPS
All:
Hail and Farewell!
The person detailed by the HPS steps forward to snuff out the East candle

In recognition that the Sabbat themes centre on the Goddess as the Earth who sustains us in life bringing forth the abundance that feeds and supports us in life as the Earth our home, the Southern Quarter is revisited:

HP and HPS stand facing South at the Southern Quarter
All move and face South again
MOC sounds the chimes three times

HP:

Once again, we do give Thanks
To the Rulers of the South and Earth
For guarding our Circle girth
And the locus of our Ritual mirth
Site of our Sabbat Rite
Hail and Farewell

Snuffer and all tools are replaced on the Altar
MOC, HP and HPS spend a short while in silence grounding, closing their eyes,
placing both hands flat on the Altar.
The coven sits on the ground. All focus in silence and ground remaining
power, channeling it into the ground, out and away.

After some minutes, the MOC sounds the smallest chime once and the HP and
HPS start the Closing Choral:

Coven joins in raising their arms in the farewell salute.
Hail and Farewell ye blessed Quarters
Fire, Air, Earth and mighty Waters
Thank you for guarding our Circle towers
And sharing of your powers

To our Lady and Lord
In love we all accord
Our thanks we give
By Your quest we live
By body, spirit, mind
Thanks for actions kind

May we always live in harmony
In Love we meet, in love we part
Blessed be!

CLEARING OF THE CIRCLE

In a similar manner as the Quarters were fare-welled in a widdershins direction,
so the Circle will be cleared in a widdershins manner.
Depending on whether it is the Light or Waxing half of the year or the Dark half
or the Waning half of the year, the HP or the HPS clears the Circle:

Light half of year: HPS,
Dark half of year: HP

The MOC sounds the gong three times.
HP or HPS stand at the Altar and present tool; raising it up on open flat palms
to eye level or higher.
HP or HPS take the Athame or Wand in both hands and walk widdershins to
the Southern Quarter {in the Southern Hemisphere/ Northern Quarter in
the Northern Hemisphere}. He/ she points the tool at the luminous line of
the scribed Circle rising from the ground forming the dome. Here, he/ she
visualizes how an invisible force beam issues forth from the tip of the tool
dispersing the light energy as they move along the Circle edge, the Circle dome
disintegrating behind them. He/ she moves from the South to the West, to the
North and the East opening and clearing the Circle boundary and the dome.
In the Northern Hemisphere he/ she would be walking from the North to the
West, on to the South, to the East and back to the North.

On arriving back at the South the HP or HPS says:

This Circle is cut!
May its blessings long remain
May we its kindness, love and essence long retain
Merry meet and merry part
And merry meet again
Blessed be!

MOC rings the gong three times
HPS says

"This Rite has ended"

Now the God and Goddess candles, the Altar work candle as well as the North
candle are snuffed

Samhain Greater Sabbat

Northern Hemisphere: 31st – 1st November
Southern Hemisphere: 30th – 1st May

Pagan New Year
Festival of the Dead
Samhuinn
Hallowe'en
All Hallowes
Calan Gaeaf
Ancestor Night
Shadowfest

SONGS/ POEMS

Celebration of the Goddess Three-fold
The Banquet of Dis
In the deepest Shadows
Hail the Ancestors

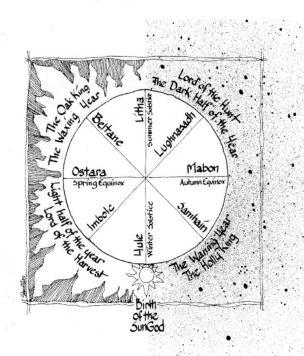

99

The Altar and Circle

This Sabbat can be celebrated inside but preferably outside, in the open around Midnight, if possible and climate permits.

Set Altar up in center of Circle so that you face East when officiating.

The Circle needs to be drawn extra large
The Altar cloth should be black with white sash

On the Altar are two pillar candles:
Orange pillar candle for the God to the left,
Orange pillar candle for the Goddess to the right
Three additional pillar candles are to be placed in the foreground of the Altar:
Three aspects of the Goddess
Maiden – white
Mother – red
Crone – black
A gold pillar candle should be located in a cauldron, located on the Altar.
A separate cauldron containing a small candle of no specific color should be placed to the side of the Altar.
As many white taper candles as there are Coveners, should be ready beside the Altar
A small loaf of bread placed on a small plate should be located to one side of the Altar.

Coveners should bring a piece of paper with an attribute, bad habit, health problem or other feature they wish to

transmute in the New Year, written on it.
Alternatively, a small box with as many pencils and papers
as there are Coveners could be located along side the Altar
Entire Coven, including HP, HPS and Master of
Ceremonies, whether male or female {MOC}, are dressed in
customary black

Other accessories:
Two taper candles, one for the HP and one for the HPS to
light the Quarter candles
Thurible/ censer with charcoal and lighter with incense
lying next to it, dishes of salt and water, chimes, symbols
for deities {e.g.:shell/ crystal and cone}
Small carafe and bowl of anointing oil, goblet of wine, bowl
of nuts
Libation dish and pentacles; one larger and a smaller on to
consecrate the salt, located in center of the Altar
BOS on stand with page weights
Sword, if applicable. Covens Wands and/ or Athames placed
on the Altar.

Samhain – Greater Sabbat

Can contain a Full Moon Rite or New Moon Rite
Insert Rite here if applicable

MOC sounds the Gong three times

Note on Widdershins Practice for Samhain:
This is the only Sabbat where it is appropriate for the Circle Casting and individual Rites to be performed in a widdershins manner, symbolic of- and consistent with the energies involving as the Earth's life force descends and the Winter Solstice is yet to take place. However, this is optional.

With the HP and HPS leading, the Coven moves deosil or widdershins if preferred, around the Circle dancing as each sees fit, faster and faster. Individual Coveners play the Triangle, Sistrum, small congas, rattles, etc, as they see fit

HP and HPS start as the Coven joins them in chanting the
The Witches' Rune
Written by Gerald Gardner and Doreen Valiente
Contained in the Gardnarian Books of Shadows, 1957
*written for Northern Hemisphere practice

Coven Call and Answer
of The Witches' Rune:

MOC, HP and HPS:
Eko, Eko...{single gong strike after each Call}

Coven chants the Covens chosen Goddess name here, of those appropriate to the Sabbat:
Diana, Inanna, Nyx, Lilith, Demeter, Dana, Hekate, Aradia, Juno, Hera, Isis, Nut, etc

MOC, HP and HPS:
Eko, Eko... {single gong strike after each Call}

Coven chants the Covens chosen God name here, or those appropriate to the Sabbat:
Herne, Pan, Cernunnos, Dis, Lugh, Pluto, Zeus, Apollo, Jupiter, Sol, Hades, Belinus, Hu the Mighty, etc

The Call and Answer of Eko, Eko can continue for several rounds as the general theme, Coven bonding and energy is established.

After the The Witches' Rune the Call and Answer of 'Eko, eko' is chanted a few times until the Singing bowl sounds 3 times over the chanting, which then dies down

HP, HPS and MOC stand at the Altar

Opening Prayer

Coven kneels on one knee forming a circle around the Altar.
HP and HP stand at Altar.
The MOC steps forward holding a taper candle and recites the prayer.
MOC:

Behold, its Samhain hour
This night of special power
We stand on the threshold between the Worlds
And feel energies beyond the Veil unfurled
It's the meeting of the Living and the Living Dead
The recollection of the done and said
Contact with family and the lives of the Past
Of flesh and blood and Circles cast
Samhain, the New Year begins in the Shadows deep
The rise and rebirth from the lowest point steep
Of potential life and latent light
Reborn at Yule and waxing bright
Its Samhain night, meeting of the world material
With the Otherworld realms ethereal
As our God and Goddess reside
Meeting in wisdom and pride
Giving each other the Gift
As each through their own Self sift
To find each other's light
In deepest mystery insight

The HPS nominates three male Coveners to each light the Goddess aspect

candles.
The Coven stands to sing:

THE CELEBRATION OF THE GODDESS THREE-FOLD

as the nominated three coveners light the candles
The three step to the Altar and with a taper candle, light each Goddess candle in turn from the already lit 'God' candle.

First Covener lighting White candle:
Goddess, Maiden fair and young
Wild of Future yet unsung
Diana, Lady of the Hunt and Forest Green
Living with beasts and seldom seen
Exploring a life free of strife
A wondrous realm enchanted
Of living things wild or planted
Of wisdom growing and expanded knowing
Of deepest insight recognition
And divine spark ignition

Second Covener lights the red candle
Goddess Grand Earth Mother
Life bearer like none other
The Grail from whence all life pours
By season cycle scores
The realms of Earth Mother Gaia
A deity none higher
The realms of Demeter Matriarch
The Womb, the Grail, the Life Spark
The Ruler of Season cycle turning
And evolving life thrust burning
The realm of Ceres Goddess Head
Ensuring that all life form 's fed
As fertile seed awaiting
For life's bounty stands equating

Third Covener lights the black candle
Our Goddess aspect Crone
By season cycle reaped the wisdom sown
Hekate, bearer of the Divine Light
Of wisdom, knowledge, insight
Hekate, guide to our Higher Self key
Light for the path leading us to see
Hekate, signpost on the forking road
Leading to our spiritual abode
Hekate, Goddess of the Mysteries Snake
Symbol of infinite cycle stake
Hekate, guardian of our psychic propylaea
The oracle for all who enquire

The Coven chants the name: Hekate!, Hekate! after every gong strike by
the MOC as the singing/ recitation ends.

The MOC steps forward with the lit taper candle.
The HP takes up the chalice of wine
HPS takes up her Athame/ Wand
HP and HPS face each other, the MOC stands to their side, with back to Altar
The MOC recites

IN THE DEEPEST SHADOWS:

In the deepest shadows resides the spark
The light that balances the dark
The air so still in Winter's blackest chill
The sun is still growing weaker
With our God aspect: Wisdom Seeker
Our Goddess with him meets
As his duality he greets
Together to share the Underworld throne
Our Goddess as Hekate Crone
They discover their binary poles

And reveal the wisdom within their dual roles
And as such they both conjoin
For latent life to coin

Athame to chalice
HP:
Light to the dark
Ignite the spark

HPS:
Seed to the earth
Cycle turns: rebirth

The three male Coveners return to their places as the the Pillar candles burn on the Altar
HPS,HP amd MOC replace their tools on the Altar. MOC motions all to sit comfortably or to lie down in a circle around the Altar. MOC sounds the smallest chimes once after all have settled:
HPS leads in quiet short Meditation:

THE BANQUET OF DIS

Let us take the steps and descend
The Banquet of Dis to attend:
Our handsome Lord Dark has bid us to hark
For we hold the Grail, he wishes avail
To his side Light of insight bright:
His Anima female side!
So, what is our Shadow dark
That beckons the lighted spark?
Let's introspect and see what's hidden that should be free;
Memories, likes, experience and traits,
That Dis can present on banquet's plates
For us to come face to face,
Know and Embrace...
Thus is the Descent and Initiation
The Dark to present by officiation

as the God and Goddess have shown
and in wisdom have grown
As a Soul united, reborn as Light-Dark polar
As Psyche respited: Luni-Solar!

*A few minutes of silence follow as all introspect and follow the idea before the
MOC sounds the smallest chimes slowly seven times.
Slowly the Coven sits up.
HPS steps forward with the cauldron containing the golden candle
The MOC lights it.*

HPS:

Here is to our God, Samhain's aspect Dark Lord
Evolved in many aspects, by Nature's Wheel scored
Born as the Sun Child, meek and mild
Slain as the Corn King for his Underworld decent
Awaiting the Goddess for introspection spent
Searching for his other side: within him it does reside!
As does the Goddess ask
Uncover my hidden other mask!
Such are our God and Goddess faces
Evolved in insight, season, cycle places
As in the deepest darkness resides light
Our God 's reborn at Yule, Sun Child bright

*HPS replaces cauldron with God candle to the front of the three burning pillar
candles representing the three aspects of the Goddess.
The Gong is struck three times*

The MOC announces
In honour of the Feast of the Dead
Let us bless and break this bread

*The HPS calls a male and female Covener
The Male Covener places the bread and the salt on the larger Pentacle
Coven stands to witness this Rite*

HPS
We commemorate our Ancestor's souls
And all we learn from their roles

On this night we feel their presence
And welcome their souls and spiritual essence

The Male Covener dips the bread into the salt:
Here is to the South, Element of Earth
Source of this bread, home of our birth
Salt of the Lake and Sea
Spice of life so free
By the Element of Water,
Symbol of our Western Quarter

Female Covener raises the Pentacle with the salted bread into the air:
Bounty of the Earth of Wealth
To keep us strong and in good health
Generated by the Cycle of the Seasons
By our God and Goddess guiding reasons

She first takes a chunk of bread crumbling it over the earth {if the Sabbat is held
outside/ placed on the libation dish if practicing inside} She then offers it to the
HP who has a bite, then to the MOC before she herself eats from it.
The Pentacle with the bread is then passed around the Circle for all to partake.

The MOC strikes the Gong three times
HPS
In memory of all deceased
We hold this Samhain Feast
We stand on the Edge of Between
And feel the souls of the entities unseen
We ponder on our family demised
Experience and wisdom highly prized
And invite here any soul so willing
To partake in our Sabbat hour, so fulfilling
Let us listen and hear
For messages from souls advancing near

HP

Let us reflect
Our abilities detect
And give Thanks to those who have gone before
For we are a product of their multiple score
And collective wisdom shared
Within us polar paired
As our God and Goddess within
Through insight learning, we win
Lets give Thanks to this special bond
Deities, Entities and Ancestors who respond
We give Thanks to these loving relations
Who inhabit Summerland's stations

Covener:
As we live our lives
Single, married, husbands, wives
We feel their presence near
Infusing confidence and banishing fear

Covener
We hear a word with an action occurred
And know that they are here
Guiding us to steer

Covener
A situation arises, an opportunity surprises
And a good deed is done
A wholesome life's run

The MOC lights three votive candles in a separate cauldron
Pencils and papers are passed around to all Coveners by the HP and HPS
The MOC strikes the Gong three times
MOC:
We look inside ourselves and choose
A Shadow to transmuse
On the paper we wish to write

What we unite by fire bright

Taper candles are passed around to all Coveners. The cauldron with the three
votive candles is placed close to the Western Quarter
One by one all Coveners start to walk deosil, or widdershins around the Circle,
they light their taper on the votive candle setting the piece of paper alight, then
dropping it into the cauldron.
The MOC walks first with the HP and HPS last, who take up position at the
Altar again. The rest of the Coven still walking deosil or widdershins.

The MOC starts The Chant:

Chant 1

Burn, Fire, burn
As we yearn
Reverse this trait
And change our fate!

Chant 2

Up in smoke it goes
To Spirit go our woes
Fire Element Transmute
Our chosen troubling attribute

Chant 3

The heat and smoke thus rises
As our trait here finally demises
And by Fire's insight flame
A new outlook we can claim

The Coven Chant fades out as it begins to sing:

HAIL THE ANCESTORS

in multiple voices while playing/ improvising on sistrums, congas, triangles,
singing bowls, tambourines, flutes, pan pipes, etc
The HP and HPS now join the Coven again
HPS starts off:
In the deepest dark burns the light

Divine spark ignite
To let us see the way
Hear our Ancestors say:
"Expand your mind
With thoughts so kind,
Open your eyes
And look beyond the rise!"

Voices 2
Feel the presence of their souls
As the leaders of past roles
Let us be open hearted
To our ancestors departed

Voices 3
Lets invite them to our Circle round
And hear their mysteries profound
Upon their sacred will
A deed for us fulfill

Voices 4
As we hear their footfalls in the snow
And we feel that hand and know
Our guides are here to show
A wisdom torrent flow

Voices 5
We are blessed with lifes' great joy
Of wisdom beauty to deploy
For upon the Sun and Moon, they shine
We see beauty clear, divine

The MOC motions for all to sit or lie down in a circle around the Altar. Then
he/ she sounds the smallest chimes once for a few minutes, if not longer, of
silence and introspection.

*Cakes and Wine/ Ale to follow
Which is in turn followed by the
Closing of the Rite*

Yule
Lesser Sabbat

Northern Hemisphere: 21st December
Southern Hemisphere: 21st June

Winter Solstice
Alban Arthuan - The Light of
Arthur

SONGS/ POEMS
The Lord of the Light Choral
Eulogy to the Sun Child
The Rule of the Oak King
Yuletide's Refrain
Hymn to Spirit

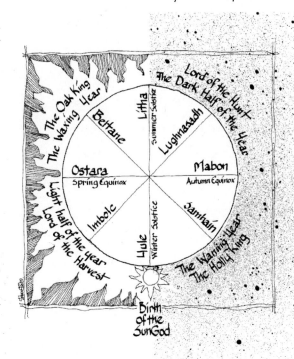

Please consult current astrological diary for the correct dates

The Altar and Circle

This Sabbat is preferably set outside, in the open at dawn, just before sunrise.
The Sabbat can be held indoors due to climatic or other reasons!

Set altar up in center of Circle so that you face East when standing at it.

The Circle needs to be drawn extra large
The Altar cloth should be purple with gold sash

On the Altar are two pillar candles:
Gold pillar candle for the God to the left,
Silver pillar candle for the Goddess to the right
Tapers of matching colors to those of the Quarter candles,
should be lying closest to the Quarter candles with an extra four candles sicks.
A large long sturdy wooden pole should have been planted/ erected at the eastern Quarter, inside the Circle.
A giant gold pillar candle placed in a cauldron stands ready on the Altar.
Chaplets or crowns of Holly and Oak, even if dormant, should be lying beside the Altar.
A dark colored veil or shawl, folded, should be placed beside the crowns.

Entire Coven, including HP, HPS and Master of Ceremonies {MOC}, whether male or female, are dressed in customary black

Other accessories:

Two taper candles, one for the HP and one for the HPS to light the Quarter candles
Thurible/ censer with charcoal and lighter with incense lying next to it, dishes of salt and water, chimes, symbols for Deities {e.g.:shell/ crystal and cone}
Small carafe and bowl of anointing oil, goblet of wine, bowl of nuts
Libation dish and Pentacles; one larger one and a smaller one to consecrate the salt located in center of the Altar
BOS on stand with page weights
Entire Covens' Athames and / or Wands to be placed on the Altar.

Yule – Lesser Sabbat
Winter Solstice

Can contain a Full Moon Rite or New Moon Rite
Insert Rite here if applicable

MOC sounds the Gong three times
With the HP and HPS leading, the Coven moves deosil around the Circle,
walking or dancing as each sees fit. Members play/ improvise on triangles,
sistrums, small congas, rattles, recorders, flutes, etc
HP and HPS start chanting the
Witches' Rune
Written by Gerald Gardner and Doreen Valiente, The Gardnarian Book of
Shadows, 1957

Once the MOC sounds the gong once, all halt and the singing of the
"Witches' Rune" ends as the Call and response of 'Eko, eko' is chanted a
few more times. Singing bowl sounds 3 times over the chanting, which then
dies down
HP, HPS and MOC stand at the Altar

Coven Chant

MOC signals for the start of the Chant
MOC:
Hail to a new Beginning
Energies of darkness thinning
For in the deepest shadows resides the spark
So, lets feel and see and hark
Our new born Sun Child burns away the dark

Walking deosil around the Circle, music is played and dies away with the start of
each Covens Chant
Covener:
It's the season of regeneration
Within the Universal station

116

Covener:
The waning year shall end
Death away to send

Covener:
The Wheel shall turn
Darkness away to burn

Covener:
It's the waxing season
Rebirth, Fauna, Flora, reason

Covener:
It's the regeneration of the Earth
The season of rebirth

Covener:
Season of growth and strength
Waxing in the six month length

Covener:
Here is to the swelling of the seed
From darkness, coldness freed

The MOC sounds the smallest chimes once as the HPS quietly starts to sing/
recite as the Coven joins in:

THE LORD OF THE LIGHT CHORAL

Arise!, awaken!, Lord of Light
Let us see Ye mild and bright
Blaze away all darkness, fear
Pour Ye forth your light so clear
Come light, come warmth, come golden ray
Come ye, to brighten up our day!

Refrain by all
Arise!, arise!, the Promised Child
Pure power undefiled

Interlude of Flute, conga drums, glockenspiel
HP continues singing
Some Coveners sing while other hum softly
Entered from the womb, life's Gateway
Arise! - the Sun to stay
Lord of the Light Year
Our Goddess Consort, Seer
The seed of renewal
Provider of warmth and fuel
Consort to Mother Earth
Locus of rebirth
Power to the Life Force
Code of Nature's Course

Opening Prayer

Some Coveners continue humming as the Gong is sounded three times
Coven kneels on one knee in the Circle around the Altar.
HP and HPS stand at Altar.
The MOC steps forward holding a taper candle and recites the prayer.
MOC:
Yule, the shortest day and longest night
The Wheel turns from darkness to the light
The energies swell in power and growth
A time to make a personal oath
Let's cast our eyes inside
And see the attributes we hide
And as the new-year waxes
At Litha it climaxes
Let us these attributes transmute
Into actions of good repute
For it is the season of renewal

On Universe's Jewel
The time for a new beginning
With life force brimming
It's the time for an inspired start
And a personal commitment smart
Energies of latent thrust
Of latent life in Earth's great crust
By our God is sown
And in our Goddess' womb is grown
For life rebirth at Yule
Upon this earthly jewel

Some Coveners improvise on Glockenspiel, sistrum and singing bowls and drums, softly.

Coven sits down and awaits the Sun's First Ray, facing due East/ Eastern Quarter

HPS says
The light brightens upon horizons line
The Child of Promise is born to shine

Chant of the Coven, one half to the beat of the Gong
Growing, growing, growing......

Seconds before the Sun's rise, some chant while others improvise on triangles, sistrums, etc
Glowing, glowing, glowing......

Sun Rise, First Ray of Yule

HP chants motioning all to rise and salute/ all join in chanting louder and louder:
Behold!, - the first Ray!
That heralds in the Season's day!
Behold!, -our Sun King!
Newborn, brightly shining!

Drums, Chimes, Gong and singing bowls as MOC locates the cauldron with extra large golden candle on the exact spot where the end of the shadow made by the pole planted at the Eastern Quarter falls to bisect the Circle on the South Western side. [in the Southern Hemisphere]

The MOC lights the candle
As the music fades, the HPS sings/ recites the

EULOGY TO THE SUN CHILD

Born of Mother Earth
The locus of our life and birth
Born from the Holy Grail
Our Child of Promise
Preparing Earth's travail
As we his Eulogy sing:
Awake! – all energies latent!
Make them manifest and patent!
Ignite! – the spark potential
For all life existential
Ignite! – the fire,
Of Earth's life giving desire
Unlock! – the life force welling
In the seed 'a swelling
And so winter demises
As Life's sap rises!

Refrain by all
Arise!, arise!, Oh Promised Child
Pure power undefiled

Part of the Coven sing in scat vocal:
Awake! – Awake! – Awake...all energeeeees...

Others sing in scat:
Ignite! - Ignite! - Ignite!...the Spark.....

All repeat refrain:
Arise!, arise!, Oh Promised Child
Pure power undefiled

The Gong is sounded three times
The MOC, HP and HPS stand at the Altar.

HPS nominates two male Coveners to act as the Oak King and Holly King.
NOTE:
The Concept of the Oak and Holly King as representing the Light and Dark half of the Year:
By Stewart and Janet Farrar
From: A Witches' Bible, Phoenix Publishing, 1981, 1984
Words by Silver Elder

HPS takes up the two wreaths and holds them over the two kneeling men's heads in front of her. She swaps them repeatedly from hand to hand before lowering one on each head.

HPS:
The Wheel of the Year has turned
The crown of the King must be earned
The scepter of power shall change hands
As energies shift across the lands
Rising with the solar arc
The sun passes the Eastern Quarter mark
Waxing year, Oh Lord of Light
Burning clear and bright
As King of the Oak
The throne is bespoke
Dying is the spark
Of our Lord of the Dark
Waning years Holly King
Has heard the death knell ring
At Litha to be reborn
After half year's sojourn

The Oak and Holly King 'do battle' around the Altar while all Coveners are
seated around the Circle periphery
Some chanting: growing, growing, growing... while others chant: glowing,
glowing, glowing....
The Holly King is 'struck down' close to the Western Quarter where he lies
'dead'. The HP and HPS 'investigate'...

HPS recites from:

THE RULE OF THE OAK KING

Behold, the Holly King has been defeated
By the Oak King, he has been unseated
His body material
Shall transmute with the earthly world
His soul ethereal
Shall pass the Veil unfurled
As he leaves the Western Portal
To be reborn immortal

The Oak King takes off the Holly King's crown and holds it up aloft in triumph.
The HPS drapes the dark scarf/ veil over the Holly King's body

The Oak King says:
Behold! Death to the year that is waning
And all energies a'draining
Welcome! - Oh Sun Child's power
At this Yuletide hour
Welcome! - the Waxing Year!
Its warmth and light so clear
With my roots deep in Mother Earth
My sap is rising in rebirth
Latent life in the Underworld
Energizing my shoot uncurled
As my sap is drawn
For life unborn

Up my tree trunk's core
Bringing budding to the fore

All chant together with the Oak King in gesture:
Clapping, tambourines, conga drums, triangles are played as Chant continues
until the Gong is struck

Draw!, draw! - up my core
From root, to shoot, to seed
Hail the waxing year, energy is freed!

The Gong is struck three times and the singing bowl is sung
The Oak King places the Holly wreath on the Altar and rejoins the Coven
The 'dead' Holly King rejoins

The MOC announces:

Five Point Star so Elemental
Air, Earth, Fire, Water, Spirit Quintessential
Elements of life giving force
Elements of Nature's Wheels resource

Covener closest to the Eastern Quarter lights a yellow taper from the Air Quarter candle, stands and
says:

Element of Air of the East
Expansive energy released
In this new Waxing Year
Air, by which light is transmitted
Air by which oxygen is acquitted
Air, vehicle of the Otherworld
Passage past the veil unfurled

Covener places the yellow candle into the candle stick on the Altar and returns to his position
Coven sings:

YULETIDE'S REFRAIN

Dark towards the light

Waxing year so bright
Birth of our Sacred Seer
From death, rebirth
Over all the Earth
'Tis the Season of Renewal
Upon Universe's Jewel
From Decline comes growth
Commitment personal oath
New life force thrust
Within Mother Earth's crust

Covener closest to the Northern Quarter lights the red taper candle from the Quarter candle, stands and

says:

Fire! - to ignite this spark
To brighten up the dark
Dispel the cold,
With sweeping warmth so bold
Ignite! - this life force
On Nature's cycle course
For insight as we know...
Occurs by Fire's lightened glow
Our Sun Child's life giving claim
Occurs by Fire's sacred flame

Covener places the red candle into the candle stick on the Altar and returns to his position

Coven sings:

YULETIDE'S REFRAIN

Covener closest to the Western Quarter lights the blue taper candle from the Quarter candle, stands and

Says:

Purest clearest Water
Symbol of our Western Quarter
Water! - the Earth to nourish

Water! – makes life flourish
Water! – infinitely mutable
Vehicle for emotions recruitable
Water, our Goddess's Element
For life so relevant

Covener places the blue candle into the candle stick on the Altar and returns to
his position

Coven sings:

YULETIDE'S REFRAIN

Covener closest to the Southern Quarter lights the green taper candle from the
Quarter candle:

Goddess, Mother Earth
The Grail, the Womb of birth
Where all Elements meet
For life's bounty replete
Nature's Cycle stage
Of infinite antiquity and age
Pentacle and Salt
Symbols by default

Covener places the green candle into the candle stick on the Altar and returns
to his position

Entire Coven sings in unison:

HYMN TO SPIRIT

And at the highest point
Of Pentagram's Star
The Arch Element anoint
With all power near and far
Is the Element Quintessential
That rules all existential
As Master of the All

Responds to beckon –call
Spirit! – Universal Director
Spirit! – mightiest protector
Spirit! – the Highest Guide
Some Coveners start to scat vocal here: Spirit!, Spirit!, Spirit!....as the
others continue to sing, recite:
Insight-intuition – Light side
Spirit, Grand Master of Creation
And all forms contemplation

Coven fades out by humming as MOC sings the largest singing bowl once and
rings the chimes once

HPS says:
Such is our living Universe
Energies focus and disperse
Energies wax and wane
Grow and drain
Such is the Law
Of the Wheel of the Year
Guiding us through Fall and Thaw
Paving a path so clear
All combines to make a Whole
The fabric of our Soul
And so we answer to Nature's draw
To see and learn much more
For we are part of the Blueprint
By Cause and Effect, Clueprint
For all we think, feel and do
Vibrates on higher planes, through and through
And by divine decree
Our eyes open up to see
And like Nature's Wheel
Lessons spool and reel
Like concept, birth, life, death, rebirth

A microcosm of Nature's life on Earth

This Rite is followed by Breakfast and Eggs with Tea and Cake
Which is in turn followed by the

Closing of the Rite

Imbolc
Greater Sabbat

Northern Hemisphere:
31st January - 1st February or 2nd February

Southern Hemisphere:
31st July - 1st August or 2nd August

The Quickening - Festival of the Light
Oimelc
Brighid's Day
Candlemas
Festival of Torches
Feast of Pan
Feast of Lights
Lupercalia

SONGS/ POEMS

The Lady of the Ice
Fire and Ice Choral
Lady of the Light Awakened
I am the Leading Light
In the Season of Rebirth

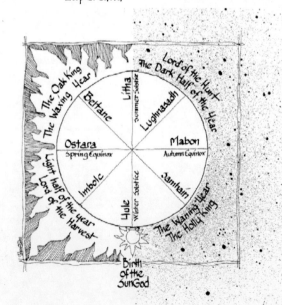

The Altar and Circle

This Sabbat is best set outside in the open at night, however if inclement weather prevails, it can just as well be held indoors!

Set Altar up in center of Circle so that you face East when officiating.

The Circle needs to be drawn extra large
The Altar cloth should be light blue

On the Altar are two pillar candles:
Gold pillar candle for the God to the left,
Silver pillar candle for the Goddess to the right
Two taper candles, one for the HP and one for the HPS to light the Quarter candles
Thurible/ censer with charcoal and lighter with incense lying next to it, dishes of salt and water, chimes, symbols for deities {e.g.:shell/ crystal and cone}
Small carafe and bowl of anointing oil, goblet of wine or soft drink, bowl of nuts or biscuits
Libation dish, Pentacles; one larger and one smaller for consecrating the salt to be located in center of the Altar
BOS on stand with page weights
Entire Covens' Athames and/ or Wands

Other accessories:
The Crown of Candles, with white candles secured in their holders, for the Imbolc Rite,
The Covens besom rests against the Altar
A cauldron containing water with dish of salt beside it. An aspergillum of herbs or other leaves in season lying beside

it.

Second Cauldron containing large white pillar candle or kindling located at the Northern Quarter

As many yellow taper candles as there are coven members.

Entire Coven, including HP {High Priest}, HPS {High Priestess} and Master of Ceremonies, whether male or female {MOC}, are dressed in customary black

Imbolc – Greater Sabbat
The Quickening – Festival of Lights

Can contain a Full Moon Rite or New Moon Rite
Insert Rite here if applicable

MOC sounds the Gong three times
With the HP and HPS leading, the Coven moves deosil around the Circle,
walking or dancing as each sees fit. Some Coveners improvise/ play the ukuleles,
bodhrán, sistrum, small congas, rattles, recorders, flutes, etc
HP and HPS start chanting or singing the
Witches' Rune
Written by Gerald Gardner and Doreen Valiente, the Gardnarian Book of
Shadows, 1957

Once all halt and the singing of the Witches' Rune ends, the Call and
response of 'Eko, eko' is chanted a few times. Singing bowl sounds 3 times over
the chanting, which then dies down.

HP, HPS and MOC stand at the Altar

Coven Call and Answer

MOC signals for the start of the Call and Answer; the Gong is rung three times.
MOC motions the Coven to walk deosil around the Circle. When requested by
the HPS individual Coveners steps forward to state their 'position'.
Some Coveners play instruments as they walk
MOC:
It's Imbolc, Greater Sabbat past Yule
Within this season of rebirth, renewal
Our Goddess quickens energy flow
So much sooner crops to sow

Covener:
Our Sun gains in light and strength
The days grow lighter, length

Slowly, slowly, Winter fades
First sightings, grassy blades

Covener:
Gently, gently, nature stirs
As evolution quietly occurs
Silent motions within the Earth so deep
Awaken from Winter's deepest sleep

Covener:
Freeze and Thaw, Freeze and Thaw
Energies swell for more
Rising sap and sprouting seed
Life's renewal is decreed

Covener:
Trickle, trickle, water's flowing
Ice is melting, Winter's going
Water, warmth and seed, earth is swelling
Life force is compelling

Covener:
Yuletide's Lady from birth recovers
Ostara – Beltane – courting Lovers
Quickening our Goddess's desires
By His ever growing solar fires

Opening Prayer

Gong strikes three blows. The MOC signals for all to kneel on one knee in a
circle around the Altar facing inwards.
The HPS leads in prayer
HPS:
Our Goddess recovers from our Sun Child's birth
Before She fully toils the earth

Though Her interest in our God is taken
She has not fully us forsaken
Quietly, Her slowly growing power
Will ensure life abundance at the growers hour
Life awakens in Earth's great crust
Seed, root and shoot breaks through the soil with thrust
Young and sprightly, fresh and clean
A new season dawns, as yet unseen
Our Goddess as awakened maiden
As yet by labours mildly laden
Stirs in waxing energies pull
To provide for barns the crop, laden full
As Winters presence quietly retreats
The weight of frosty darkness finally depletes

HP and HPS sing:

THE LADY OF THE ICE

Some Coveners accompany the singing while others hum of play instruments
eg: Flute, recorder, oboe
Hail! – Our Lady of the Ice!
In Her aspect, triple, thrice
Season of the Maiden, pure
To winters darkness, cure

Here some Coveners sing in scat vocal: Hail! – Hail! – Hail!...while other
continue singing/ reciting:
Fertility and life by melted waters
Symbol of our Western Quarters
Into Earth it saturates and seeps
Germination from Winter's sleeps

HPS sings:
Hail! – Our God of Solar Fire

Free this Earth from darkness, mire
Here some Coveners sing in scat vocal: Hail! – Hail! – Hail!...while other
continue singing/ reciting:
By Flame to cleanse the fields
For bounty harvest yields
By Fire, from Water's grip release
And by light all darkness, cease

The Gong rings three times, the humming and scat vocal fades
The MOC requests the HPS to appoint a Covener to light the candle or
kindling prepared in the cauldron located at the Northern Quarter. While this
is happening, the Coven stands and starts moving deosil past the Altar where
the HPS hands out yellow tapers, to all male Coveners, the HP to all female
Coveners.

MOC introduces

Let the energies strengthen as the days now lengthen
We sense and feel the energies accrued
As the ice does melt in cold and frosty blue
Crackling, crawling stirrings, little by little
The Earth is freed by Nature's Wheels acquittal
And as the life force swells, unfolds
Roots and buds burst from Winter moulds
The energies transform within the seed and corm
As the melting waters purify
And the Earth soil thereby nourify
The Earth from winter's frost grip freed
Living stirrings within plant, beast and seed

Dancing and chanting, singing in choral starts as directed by the MOC as the
Coveners move deosil past the Altar, to first; light their candles from the
Goddess candle if male, the God candle if female. Each Covener then circles the
Circle once and during the second full circle, drops the candle into the cauldron
to feed the fire.

Coven sings, in many voices

FIRE AND ICE CHORAL

Choral 1

Lord of the Fire
Melt away this Winter's cold
On your blazing pyre
Sweep away the old
And usher in the new
Let energy grow, accrue

Choral 2
Lady of the Ice
By Season's roll of dice
By melted waters pure
Pave the way
For Winter's cure
By ever waxing day
And growing light so sure

Choral 3
As Fire and Ice they meet
As the waxing year they greet
Cleansed and purified and blessed
The Goddess shall return from rest

Choral 4
Fire and Ice and Earth
To generate rebirth
With germination to ensue
Life force will accrue

The Gong rings three times

The HP and the HPS are the last to drop their candles into the cauldron
The MOC awaits them at the Altar. The MOC hands the Coven's besom to the
HPS who in turn hands it to the HP. The HP dances in theatrical fashion around
the circle making sweeping motions with the besom while the Coven, seated
around the Circle periphery chants and claps faster and faster. HP dances faster
and faster, spinning about.
Coven in many voices:

Chant 1

Sweep, sweep away the Winter sleep
Usher in the new
Manifest by life that's due

Chant 2

Sweep, sweep in new life steep
Freed from Winter's cold
Banished to the old

Chant 3

Sweep, sweep Winter's darkness creep
Awaiting Summer's toil
In ever fertile soil

Chant 4

Sweep, sweep towards Ostara's neap
All darkness to vanish
All cold to banish

The Gong is sounded three times
The HPS stands with back to the Altar in Osiris pose, with Athame and Wand crossed.
The entire Coven, except for the HP, HPS and MOC sing in choir as the Candle Crown is very slowly lowered over the HPS's head. The MOC slowly lights one candle after another, with a taper lit from the God candle on the Altar. Once all candles are lit, he slowly draws the invoking Pentagram of the Earth in the air over the crown.
Coven as Choral Choir, repeat three times sings:

LADY OF THE LIGHT AWAKENED

Oh Lady of the Light, come hither
Make the darkness wither
Oh, Lady of the Light shine brightly
For love requitely
Oh, Lady of the Light, see the Winter through

Melt the frost of blue
For rebirth renew
Oh, Lady of the Light, come and blaze the Way
With ever lengthening day
Swing in summer sway
Swing in here to stay
Oh, Lady of the Light, turning Nature's Wheel
For Winter to repeal
And our harvest fate to seal

HPS slowly opens into Isis/ blessing pose, holding Athame and Wand aloft in salute

She recites:

I AM THE LEADING LIGHT

I am the leading light
The warming spark ignite
Arisen from the Winter ashes
As by fleeting flashes
Dark departs
The waxing year here starts
Ice and snow will melt
Waxing warmth is felt
I will burn the blazing trail
And to the God I shall avail
Come Ostara, Beltane, Litha season
For we shall wed for harvest reason
In my name
For all harvest abundance
And earthly fecundance
And by Grail decreed
Life! – to Earth and seed

The HPS kisses the blade of her Athame and replaces it and the wand on the Altar

She presents and then scrapes some salt onto the smaller pentacle alongside the larger one.

HP presents and then holds his Athame in clasped hands with point over the salt

HP says:

Product of the Earth
Locus of our birth
Sacred and pure
Free from Evil allure
So mote it be!

HPS first presents then places the cauldron of water on the larger Pentacle

HPS presents and then holds her Athame in clasped hands with tip over the water

HPS:

Product of the All
Manifest by Earths cry call
Element of renewal regeneration
For life's sacred veneration
So mote it be!

HPS scoops three Athame tips of salt into the Water and swirls three times deosil

HPS:

Sacred, pure and blessed
May the God and Goddess be addressed
Healthy in body, pure in heart, positive in mind
To live and love and do deeds kind
So mote it be!

HPS holds the cauldron high up into the air and says:

To our God and Goddess
To life and love
Blessed be!

HPS replaces the cauldron on the Pentacle

HP takes it up. HPS along side him, uses the aspergillum of herbs to sprinkle all male Coveners filing past the Altar, lastly she sprinkles the HP and MOC {if male}. The HP sprinkles all female Coveners and the MOC {if female} and

lastly, the HPS.
As each Covener passes, the MOC recite:
In this season of rebirth
May it be one of love and mirth
In this season of renewal
May it be one of visionary accrual
In this season of waxing light
May it be one of gaining sight
In this season of quickening growth
May it be one of personal oath
In this season of yearning
May it be one of deeper learning!

This Rite is followed by Cakes and Wine/ Ale
Which is in turn followed by the
Closing of the Rite

139

Ostara/ Eostre
Lesser Sabbat

Northern Hemisphere: 21st March
Southern Hemisphere: 21st September

Spring Equinox - Vernal Equinox
Alban Eilir - Light of the Earth
Lady Day
Eostra's Day

SONGS/ POEMS

Return of the Goddess
Ode to Life Force
I am Ostara Spring
Blessing the Elements

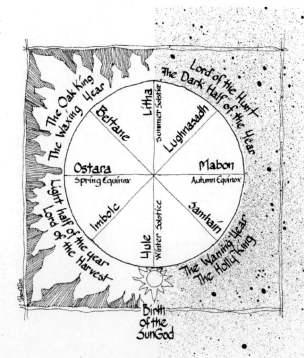

Please consult current astrological diary for correct dates

The Altar and Circle

This Sabbat can be set outside in the open just after sunrise, or indoors if weather is an issue.

Set Altar up in center of Circle so that you face East when officiating.
The Circle needs to be drawn extra large
The Altar cloth should be light green

On the Altar are two pillar candles:
Gold pillar candle for the God to the left,
Silver pillar candle for the Goddess to the right
The largest cauldron filled with earth and freshly germinated grass should be located on the center of the Altar. A large gold pillar candle should be located in the center of the cauldron.
As many pencils and papers as there are members of the Coven.
A folded light blue shawl should be located beside the altar.
The circle periphery should be decorated with flowers in season, particularly daffodils as they are gold/ yellow
The Coven, including the Master of Ceremonies {MOC}, whether male or female, are dressed in customary black.
Option: HP and HPS could be dressed in white with the HP wearing a yellow or gold colored tabard over his robe.

Other accessories:
Two taper candles, one for the HP and one for the HPS to light the Quarter candles
Thurible/ censer with charcoal and lighter with incense lying alongside it, dishes of salt and water, chimes and Gong hanging in stand.

Symbols for deities {e.g.:shell/ crystal and cone}
Small carafe and bowl of anointing oil, goblet of wine, bowl
of nuts or plate of cakes
Libation dish and both Pentacles; a larger one and the
smaller one for consecrating the salt to be located in center
of the Altar
BOS on stand with bookmark page weights
Covens' Athames and/ or Wands

Ostara/ Eostre – Lesser Sabbat
Spring Equinox

Can contain a Full Moon Rite or New Moon Rite
Insert Rite here if applicable

MOC sounds the Gong three times
With the HP and HPS leading, the Coven moves deosil around the circle,
walking or dancing as each sees fit. Some improvise or play instruments as they
see fit.
HP and HPS start dancing while chanting or singing the
Witches' Rune
Written by Gerald Gardner and Doreen Valiente, the Gardnarian Book of
Shadows, 1957

Once all halt and the singing of the Witches' Rune ends, the Call and
Response of 'Eko, eko' is chanted a few times.
The MOC sounds the singing bowl 3 times over the chanting, which then dies
down
HP, HPS and MOC stand at the Altar

Coven Call and Answer

MOC signals for the start of the Call and Answer by ringing the chimes
MOC motions all to walk deosil around the circle. When requested by the HPS,
individual Covener begins to recite.
Some Coveners play instruments or hum as they walk.

MOC:
It's a wondrous time of year
As we align with life force near
We sense and feel her song
And hear her strike the gong
Hark! – Hark!
It's the Midway mark
Of the year in light
As Ostara bright

Some Coveners repeat in refrain: Hark! – Hark!, – its the Midway mark...

Covener:
Light and power increase
As frost and coldness cease
In lighter green the land is dressed
Warmth and light by sun invest

Some Coveners repeat in refrain: Hark! – Hark!, – its the Midway mark...

Covener:
The sun is higher on the solar arc
Standing at the equidistant mark
Of equal night and day
Onwards, the solar quarter way

Some Coveners repeat in refrain: Hark! – Hark!, – its the Midway mark...

Covener:
Energies dip t'wards the light
Gaining power in warmth and bright
Enveloped in growth and green
A spectacle as yearly seen

Some Coveners repeat in refrain: Hark! – Hark!, – its the Midway mark...

Covener:
Waters from the ice are freed
Feeding life in seed
Midway in the waxing year
Quickening life force clear

Some Coveners repeat in refrain: Hark! – Hark!, – its the Midway
mark...
By now more Coveners softly sing in scat as background to the recitation
and the refrain: Midway mark, mark... mark..., Midway mark,
midway...midway...

Covener:
In his youthful adolescence
Our Sun God makes his presence
By stronger suns ray
To herald in the way
For his Litha climax
At season's full wax

Refrain and scat vocal

Covener:
As One is the Whole and the Whole forms One
Our Goddess' soul is nourished by the Sun
As growth all round abounds
In all of life resounds

Refrain and scat vocal

Covener:
Myriad of scents and smells
Cast Ostara's spells
Opposing colors in light and shade
By our God and Goddess made

Refrain and scat vocal

Covener:
As polar forces here combine
By Goddess aspect trine

As Ostara's maiden nature bound
Creation's life force in sight and sound

Refrain and scat vocal

Covener:
Our Goddess is elected
The our Sun God directed
In beauty bounty to grow and swell
To Winter's cold and darkness quell

During the Coven's Call and Answer, the HPS goes to kneel under her shroud of light blue at the Eastern Quarter. She is surrounded by flowers scattered around her, notably yellow, golden ones, such as daffodils.
Soft conga drum beat with ever increasing bass bongo drums in background.
Glockenspiel by the MOC signals end to all music.

MOC sings/ recites, with part Coven accompaniment, while others hum:

RETURN OF THE GODDESS

Behold the calmness of the lake
The beckoning words our Lady spake:
"I shall return!" she said
To provide the life force, fed
From Yule's Sun Child well recovered
And Imbolc's lusting boy well mothered
Our Goddess to Earth returns
As the sun ever stronger burns
Behold, the Lady of the Lake has entered
Via the Eastern Portal centered
Freed at the Underworld gateway, symbol of our Western
Quarter
Our Lady of the Lake and Water
Released from Water's ice
As Maiden, Goddess aspect thrice

From her Winter's sojourn she arises
Rebirth, her creation now comprises
Mother of the Energy flow
To till, to seed, to sow

Coven in fade out refrain and scat vocal: To till, to seed, to sow! - to
till, to seed, to sow...

HP sings/ recites
Conga drums and guitar accompany humming and singing
As One is in All and All is in One
Our God has brightened up the Sun
For life springing from the Earth
The locus of rebirth
And from Winter's ice now freed
Our Lady's energies for life decreed
Slowly she arises from the deep
From her Underworld mystery keep
From the stillness silver blue
She steps to land, for life force new
As via the universal womb
She is reborn from her Underworld tomb
Via Water's Portal, the Lakes
Her entrance here she makes
As our God awaits her at the shore
As the Sun, as reeds, as rushes, more

HPS, kneeling at the Eastern Quarter candle slowly draws back the shawl and
drapes it around her shoulders.
She gathers up as many flowers as she can grasp with both hands and rises to
stand in the Osiris pose; both forearms crossed on the chest.
HPS sings:

I AM OSTARA SPRING

Behold!, I am the life force of Ostara Spring

The energies of life I bring
Life force of Water, Air and Light
Life force of evolving might
Life force forming within the ground
Life force above and all around
Life force high within the planes
Life force that waxes, wanes
I am Manifestation and Creation
I am Concept and Emanation
I am the living principle
I am the rebirth cycle invincible
I am Natures Soul
The All in One that forms the Whole
I am the life giver of the Universe
I am the emanator of energies disperse
I am the life force Elemental
I am existence transcendental
I am the thought form ethereal
And Law manifestation material

Part of the Coven start singing in scat vocal: Life!- Life! - Life force...
Others sing/ scat: I am! – I am! – I am! – ....

Finally, all sing in scat as powerfully as possible, ending with a long drawn out:
Life Force!...

HPS opens up in Isis pose; the blessing pose, holding the flowers high in the air.
Flowers are scattered on the ground all around her.
Coven quietly starts singing in choral becoming stronger and stronger:

ODE TO LIFE FORCE

Choral 1
From seed, to bud, to shoot
Life sap rises from the root

Through stem, to leaf, to flower
In energizing power

Choral 2
It's the Season of the Stag
After Winter's dreary lag
Antlers in velvet cover
Consort to the Goddess, lover

Choral 3
Our God in many guises
As Sun and Green Man he comprises
God and Goddess binary pair
Both for life on Earth declare

Choral 4
It's the Season of giving strength
Life force goes the extra length
In quickening cycle evolution
In tune with Nature's cycle Earth solution

Choral 5
Our Goddess arisen beckons- calls
To our Sun God from winters palls:
"Come hither! - sacred seed of light,
Enliven and enlighten this Earth so bright!"

Choral 6
Renewal on Earth ensure
By Divine energies so pure
By the Sun Gods ever growing glow
We shall reap what we will sow

Song quietly fades out. The gong is struck three times
MOC leads in prayer as HP and HPS hand out pencils and paper to all Coveners
as they walk deosil around the Circle. As they pass the Altar, the HP hands

pencil and paper to female Coveners and the HPS to all male Coveners.

Prayer

MOC leads
Our Lord and Lady, hear us speak
For it is your guidance that we seek
We also wish here Thanks to give
For all guidance by which we learn and live
For awakening the divine
Within our heart
For surmounting the incline
By lessons you impart
We give Thanks for insight and strength
For visions that enlight
To take us that extra length
We give Thanks for the silver cord
And having you aboard
On our astral trips and seeing Past Life clips
We give Thanks for being shown the way
And taught each day
We give Thanks for all clues
And to our questions, all the news
We give Thanks for each magickal event
And all inspiration Spirit sent.

The Coven is seated in a circle, looking inwards towards the Altar
All including the MOC, HP and HPS write a wish on the paper.
After a few minutes of introspection and silence, the MOC sounds the gong
three times.

HP
Lord and Lady hear us speak
It is your guidance that we seek
For we have an Ostara wish
To plant in this Ostara cauldron dish

HPS lights the candle in the cauldron

HP
For like the seed in nurtured soil shall grow
We write our wish, and by actions we shall know
It's resonated on the higher planes
To manifest in Earth's domains
For like a seed, our wish we plant
With a quiet prayer and song and chant

HPS
And by the candle light and heat
With Spirit our wish shall meet
It's a special favour, which we ask
To inspire our burden task
And we shall wait and see for outward action
If our wish has met with traction

Coveners walk deosil around the Circle, past the cauldron standing on the Altar
where they 'dig' the small folded paper into the soft soil around the candle.
The MOC, HP and HPS 'plant' their seed wish last
Once all wishes are 'planted', the HP and HPS appoint two male and two female
Coveners to bless the wish cauldron
As the appointed Coveners bless the 'planted' wishes in the Cauldron, the rest
of the Coven sing, while some hum:

BLESSING OF THE ELEMENTS

Female Covener - Air
Give our wishes wings to fly
May they in virtue multiply
On Air's ethereal planes supreme
May our psychic visions stream
In constant motion atom movement
May our wishes find divine approvement
As by higher level correspondence

Our thought forms find respondence
On Earth to find a physical form
And become a manifested norm

Female Covener - Fire

By Fire's blessings, make these wishes come alive
Infuse them with power, light and drive
Let us feel that inner spark
That heralds from the dark
As these wishes turn to motion
Stirred, enlivened by divine devotion
Let us feel that sacred glow
That confirms to us; "we know!"
Our wish has come to being
To all hearts ever seeing

Male Covener – Water

By Water's blessings keep our emotions pure
As by Salt, all evil shall be cure
As by Water blessed, evil to good transmute
For actions, deeds of good repute
Make us feel our wishes granted
As by this seed today here planted
Wash away all sadness feelings
And all distressed past reelings
Let clear emotions flow
For our wishes' seed to grow

Male Covener - Earth

Gateway between the Worlds and our life's locus
Venue of Nature's Wheel in focus
Place of synthesis and Spiritual boundary
Of our time- space learning foundry
The Earth, the Goddess womb
And our future bodies tomb

Venue of our material birth and ritual mirth
The place of material incarnation
Ere moving to the higher station
Bless our wishes planted in its soil
May they grow by Spirit's toil

Entire Coven chants:
By Air, by Earth, by Water, by Fire
Make manifest our wished desire
Fulfill our dreams
For kind thought streams
To enrich our lives
For higher strives
For love to offer
And help to proffer
For eyes to see
And wisdom decree
For a heart to feel
Good thoughts to seal
To make us whole
Past wrongs console

This Rite is followed by Cakes and Wine/Ale
Which is in turn followed by the Closing of the Rite

Beltane
Greater Sabbat

Northern Hemisphere: 30th April - 1st May
Southern Hemisphere: 31st October - 1st November

Bealteinne
Festival of the Flowering
May Day
Walpurgisnacht
Calan Mai
Céitein
Festival of Tana

SONGS/ POEMS

The Beltane Love Chase
The Bel-Fire Blaze
I am the Stag
Rejoice! - The Lord and Lady
Burn, Burn - Let the Cycle turn
Lady of the Waxing Year
I am She

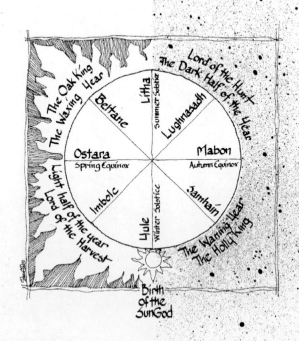

The Altar and Circle

This Sabbat is best set at mid-morning, outside in the open.
Indoors is just as appropriate in event of bad weather.

The Circle needs to be drawn extra large
Set altar up in center of Circle so that you face East when
officiating.
The May Pole with alternating white and red ribbons is
located near the Eastern Quarter
The Cauldron containing kindling representing the Bel-Fire
is located near the Northern Quarter
The outer edge of the Circle and the Altar should be
decorated with flowers that are in season
The Altar cloth should be bright green

On the Altar are two pillar candles:
Gold pillar candle for the God to the left,
Silver pillar candle for the Goddess to the right
One additional shorter larger green pillar candle stands on
the God side of the Altar, symbolizing EARTH
Crowns/ chaplets lie beside the Altar:
Crowns of Wattle flowers and Eucalyptus leaves for the HPS
and all female Coveners
A crown of Oak leaves/ shoots for all male coveners
As many wax taper candles as there are members in the
Coven lie to one side of the Altar.
The 'cakes' should be a bowl of nuts

Other accessories:
Two taper candles, one for the HP and one for the HPS to
light the Quarter candles
Thurible/ censer with charcoal and lighter with the incense

alongside it, dishes of salt and water, chimes, symbols for deities {e.g.:shell/ crystal and cone}
Small carafe and bowl of anointing oil, goblet of wine, bowl of nuts
Libation dish near the God candle, one smaller Pentacle to consecrate the salt and a larger one located in center of the Altar
BOS on stand with page weights
Entire Covens' Athames and/ or Wands are presented on the Altar

Beltane – Greater Sabbat

NOTE:
The Concept of the Love Chase as a seasonal motif was inspired by:
Stewart and Janet Farrar
From: A Witches' Bible, Phoenix Publishing, 1981, 1984
Words by Silver Elder

The HP, HPS and MOC stand at the Altar and face Coven casually standing
around the Circle
The smaller singing bowl is rung three times by MOC
Some Coveners drum softly on bodhráns, congas, etc

MOC says:
Attention all, it's the Sabbat meet
Joy of Soul and flight of feet
Love in heart and pure in mind
Here to meet in spiritual kind

HPS:
Off to the Sabbat meet we go
For love and light to sow

All:
Here's to the Sabbat meet
In love to greet

HP raises his arms in greeting
MOC rings the chimes again, three times

HP says:
We call upon the Lady of the Greenwood, wild and free
Goddess of love and fertility
We wish to feel You live in presence
In Your love and power effervescence

All:

Blessed Be!

HPS raises her arms in greeting
MOC rings the chimes again three times
HPS says:
I call upon the Lord of the Greenwood
Pan of the Forest and The Horned One
God the Waxing Year
We invite You here
To rejoice in Your presence
And your glory effervescence

All:
Blessed be!

HP and HPS raise their arms in greeting
In unison the HP and HPS say:
Hail to the Sabbat of Beltane
Time for love and joy spontane
We celebrate the Lady and Lord
And their union in divine accord
For the two are One
And One is the All
We harken for their loving Call

With the HP and HPS leading, the Coven moves deosil/ sunwise around the
Circle, walking or dancing as each sees fit while some Coveners improvise/ play
instruments as they see fit.
HP and HPS start and all join in chanting the
The Witches' Rune
Written by: Gerald Gardner and Doreen Valiente for the Gardnarian Book of
Shadows in 1957.

Eventually all halt and the singing ends as the call and response of 'Eko, eko' is
chanted a few times
MOC sounds the gong three times over the chanting which then dies down
MOC, HP and HPS stand at the Altar

The HP steps forward and addresses the Coven standing in a circle facing inward

THE LADY CHANT

HP:

The Lady hath set Her foot upon the path
To create a home and hearth
In the Lover-Mother aspect, Hers
New responsibility confirs

The HPS steps forward standing alongside the HP:

THE LORD CHANT

HPS:

The Lord hath reached His journeys end
And decided for more time to spend
For with our Lady He's conjoined
And on this day, new life is coined

*Seasonal motif enactment follows as the HPS and HP enact the Love Chase
around the Circle
Coven splits in two voice choral while the Chase is going on. Coveners
improvise/ play instruments as they wish.
Choral 1 sings* 'THE LADY' *rhyme above*
Choral 2: sings 'THE LORD' *rhyme above*
*The HP and HPS weave in between the Coveners who are standing in a Circle,
jazz broom on drum and singing in refrain
The MOC sounds the gong three times and signals for the designated Covener
to recite the theme:*
Covener recites:

THE BELTANE LOVE CHASE

Let us say farewell to dark
And see the ever brightening spark
Growing ever warmer in its glow
Nature's cycle's in the know
The sun rises higher overhead

Germination in good stead

The cycle's wheel is turning
Our Lady's heart is yearning
Its is the season of love and joy and sharing
Its is the season, Lord and Lady pairing
Here is to life, to love and lust
And all in life's great cause that's just

After several laps of the HPS and HP chasing in the Circle, the HPS allows
herself to be captured, embraced and kissed by the HP.
The HP and HPS choose the next couple to chase, who in turn choose the next
until all Coveners had a chance. In all cases the female should allow herself to be
captured, embraced and kissed consistent with the theme of the Sabbat. Those
who have completed the Chase start to sing the Choral below and improvise/
play instruments to accompany the singing:

ON THIS DAY OF BELTANE

Coven Choral refrain 1
Both young and free
Our Lord and Lady
On this day conjoin
A new life to coin
God of the Greenwood
Union understood

A few Coveners sing in scat vocal: Life! - Life! - Life!....Life to coin...
{the word 'coin' is drawn out}

Coven Choral refrain 2
Love and Life this day
The Rites of passage way
In love and joy
It'll be a boy
Yule, his birth date

New born God state

A few Coveners sing in scat vocal: Love! – Love! – Love! ....Love and Joy...{ the word 'Joy' is drawn out}

Coven Choral refrain 3
God of the Waxing Year
Longer days bright and clear
Our Lord begins to feel
A relationship to seal
Emotions from his heart
A new life to start

A few Coveners sing in scat vocal: Love! – Love! – Love! ....Love and Joy...{ the word 'Joy' is drawn out}

Coven Choral refrain 4
This day we celebrate
Conjoined, they will procreate
New life blood as they mate
New life in joy and love
Blessings all around, above

A few Coveners sing in scat vocal: Love! – Love! – Love! ....Love and Joy...{ the word 'Joy' is drawn out}

Coven Choral refrain 5
The God's new shepherd role
Stirring feelings in his soul
For a new life to care
Growing conscious and aware
No longer quite so free
In his lover's seeking spree

A few Coveners sing in scat vocal: Love! – Love! – Love! ....Love and

Joy...{ the word 'Joy' is drawn out}

Coven Choral refrain 6
On this day of Beltane
We sing this short refrain
Love is the cycle of life
Child, Maiden Goddess-Wife
Here is to our Lord of the Forest-Oak
With horns and green his cloak
He has planted the seed
For a new life to breed

All sing in scat vocal: Love! - Love! - Love! ....Love and Joy...{ the
word 'Joy' is drawn out}
Some Coveners for a rhythmic scat of: Joy! - Joy! - Joy!
All in fade out: Love and Joy...drawn out with singing bowl
accompaniment

Call and Answer

The MOC strikes the gong three times.
HP and HPS signal for all to sit down. The HPS starts the Beltane Call and
Answer. Both the HP and HPS randomly appoint Coveners to 'answer'
illustrating the themes of Beltane.

THE BEL-FIRE BLAZE

Is recited as a call and answer
HPS says:
It is the turning of the Wheel
For new life to seal
It's the Lord's journey's end
For more time to spend
A time to share and cleave
By coupling to conceive

162

Covener:
Time the soil to nourish
For Nature here to flourish
Time to plant the seed
For new life to breed
As the days grow longer
And the life force stronger

The HPS appoints a male Covener to light the Earth candle on the Altar.
Male Covener takes a working taper on the Altar, lights it on the God candle
and in turn lights the Earth candle

HPS:
At Yule, the Oak King has re-awakened...
Winter's cold and darkness is forsaken

Female Covener appointed by HPS:
God of the waxing year
Free from cold and fear
Time to fertilize the fruit
In seed, bud and shoot

Male Covener at Altar with Earth Candle:
Here is to birth
And Earth's great mirth
Here is to the young
And life as yet unsung

HP:
In our Gods' loving great embrace
New love and life we face

Entire Coven sings with the HPS as lead vocal
HPS:
Time to light the Bel-fire bright
To be near and far in sight

Let the flames grow higher
In passion and desire
And here we hark
In every flicker spark
A new kindling life force
Free from sadness and remorse

Part of the Coven hums while a few voices sing a scat-vocal of :
Time to light, Time to light, Bel-Fire bright, Bel-Fire bright,
Light, Light, the Bel-Fire,
Bel-Fire, bright, bright...

The MOC sounds the smallest chimes once and signals for all Coveners to file
past the Altar in a deosil direction where the HPS is handing out tapers which
the Coveners light on the green Earth candle. The scat vocal of: 'Light Light
Bel-Fire Bright...' continues

THE BEL-FIRE BLAZE

HPS starts the recitation as she leads the Coven deosil around the Circle where
one by one they drop their lit candles into the cauldron filled with kindling at
the Northern Quarter.

HPS begins:
Its time to light
The Bel-fire bright
On each and every hill top
To energize the crop
For a bumper harvest time
In warmer spring time clime
As our Lord and Lady cleave
And new life they conceive

All dance and run faster and faster following the HPS as she takes a leap over
the fire on the cauldron. One by one all leap the burning cauldron.

The MOC sounds the gong once. The dancing dies down and the MOC divides
the Coven into two groups to sing or recite while others play/ improvise on
instruments.

Coven choral 1
Stoke the Bel-fire bright
Here is to the Beltane Rite
In its golden glow
We'll reap and we'll sow
Here is to Nature's Wheel
That annual fate to seal
Product of the love chase
On this day, this place

Coven choral 2
Rejoice and cleave as One
As our Lord and Lady've done
Each new seed is to imbue
With new life force to ensue

Coven choral 3
Stoke that Bel-fire high
And feel our Lord and Lady nigh
Here is to the new creation story
In all its natural glory

Coven choral 4
Stoke this Beltane-Fire
Let the sparks drift higher
Upon near and distant hills
Our Lord, his seed he spills
Gone are the winter chills

Coven choral 5
Summer is a reckoning
The Kingship is a beckoning
Beltane, God and Goddess wild
Conceiving of their love life child

HP says:

Nature's turning wheels
Many a fate it seals

Coven:

Moon and solar cycle seasons
Natures ebb and tide and reasons

HPS says:

Farewell, our Lord as Winter's dark half ends
Hail, our Lady as light half year she spends

Coven:

Farewell to the Winter dark and cold
Our Lord, loving, strong and bold

HP:

As the sun moves further East
The length of day increased
The day that's spent in longer light
Hail our Lady in love so bright

Coven:
Hail and Farewell

HP:
Hail and Farewell

HPS:
Hail and Farewell

HP,HPS and MOC return to the Altar. Coven stand around the Circle. The HP and HPS stand and face one another. The MOC sounds the gong slowly and repeatedly as the HPS hands the HP the already lit Earth candle. The HP receives it, turns and faces the Coven as he steps forward. He holds it up high and recites theatrically:

I AM THE STAG

I am the stag in the gloaming forest glen
I am the little Fairy wren
I am the seed spill't
In the fertile river silt
I am the warming Sun's rays
The life giving warmth blaze
I am the scented flowers
And the nourishing rainy hours
I am the soaring eagle high
And the chirping cricket nigh
I am the wakening Earth's crust
Of fertile vigorous lust
I am the rain cloud ever swelling
And the flowing creek source welling
I am the pollen carrying gentle breeze
And the shelter in wind swept plains and lees
I am the promise of the sap rising
As the cold and frost of winter is demising

The MOC sounds the chimes and the HP replaces the Earth Candle on the Altar
and takes up a Wattle flower and Eucalyptus leaf wreath and presents it. The
HPS kneels facing the coven while the HP slowly lowers it with both hands onto
her head.
While this is happening, the MOC recites

LADY OF THE WAXING YEAR

Onwards, upwards towards the light
Litha's near and within our sight
Our Lord and Lady, bride
Pregnant by his side
All in One and One in All
Awaiting our God and Goddess call

Through them we see with inner eye
As our inner soul we scry
And find the true path to our inner Self
Our unconscious commonwealth
As light meets dark
There ignites a spark
Of true divine cognition
And new life path transition

A covener in the background rises says theatrically:
Hark, we hear our Lady's call
Through mundane's material pall
Present in our Circle Rite
In flesh and blood and sight

The HPS steps forward facing the Coven as she moves to stand with legs astride
in Isis pose, arms in the air outstretched.
The HPS lowers her arms and spreads them wide to the Coveners standing
around the Circle edge.
HPS recites:

I AM SHE

I am She who turns the Wheel
Which many a fate does seal
As the season comes and goes
And living program knows
I germinate the seed
For all new life decreed
As by our God new life I bear
A life so innocent and fair
Cleave- conjoin in my name
As follows Nature's cycle, same
Ye shall love all life
And live it without strife
Live the role for others

Your sisters and your brothers
Ye shall sow the seed of joy
Which naught other can destroy
For I will be your constant guide
For ever within ye, by your side
As the God lives within me
For He is me and I am He
For so above and so below
As the correspondences go
For All is the One and I am the All
The Quintessential Material
Earthly and Ethereal
Matter Universal
By divine dispersal

MOC stands at the Altar and sounds the gong three times.

REJOICE!-THE LORD AND LADY

MOC announces:
Let us rise and celebrate
As our Lord and Lady procreate
In love and joy to dance
In ecstatic lively trance
And from the hill tops expound the news
Our God has found his loving muse
The crops shall grow again
In fertile lands and nourishing rain

The Bel-Fire cauldron is burning at the Northern Quarter while the May Pole
stands near the Eastern Quarter
Both the HP and HPS, wearing their wreaths are standing at the altar signalling
the coveners to file past. The MOC sounds the smallest chimes slowly in
succession. Each Female covener steps to the altar and kneels as the HP places a
Wattle-flower and Eucalyptus wreath with both hands upon her head. The HPS
places an Oak wreath with both hands upon each kneeling male covener.

The May Pole Dance

The MOC sounds the gong three times and the HPS signals all to follow her as
she leads them deosil to the May-Pole
Each of the coveners takes a ribbon [males: red, females: white] and dances
around the pole with it, intertwining one with another.
This is continued until all ribbons are tied around the pole, symbolizing the
union of male and female, the joining of all together.
The Coven chant-sings:

BURN! BURN!, - LET THE CYCLE TURN:

Celebrate the Beltane time of year
Betwixt Ostara and Litha clear
Celebrate the Bel-Fire's might
As we dance all night
Here's to growth out on the land
By divine intent as planned
Here's to growth within our heart
Beltane night, its time to start
As our Lord to introspect departs
Ponders his Goddess aspect arts
Our Lady bears his seed and cell
A new life, healthy, strong and well
New life force, blood and plasma
New sun course, seed, phantasma
Burn, Burn – let the Cycle turn
Root and bud and fruit
Lamb and calf and foal
Growth on land and in our soul
Onward walk the path in vigor zest
Living by our sacred quest

On completion of all the ribbons being tied around the May Pole, part of the
Coven chant/ sing in scat vocal a few more times:

Life! Life! Life! ...Life Force!

Another part of the Coven reply in scat vocal: New Sun Course,... New Sun Course...

Finally, all chant :
New Life Force: Blood and Plasma!
New Sun Course, Seed, Phantasma!

The Coven chants a few times before the MOC sounds the gong for Cakes and Wine:

This Rite is followed by Cakes and Wine/ Ale
Which is in turn followed by the
Closing of the Rite

Litha
Lesser Sabbat

Northern Hemisphere: 21st June
Southern Hemisphere: 22nd December

Summer Solstice – Midsummer
Alban Heruin – Light of the Shore

SONGS/ POEMS

The Wedding of the Gods
At Zenith's Peak
Blessed Sacred Waters
The Holly King's Rule

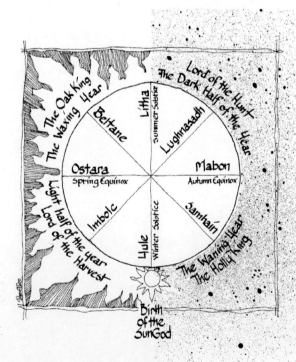

Please consult current astrological diary for the correct dates

The Altar and Circle

This Sabbat is best held late morning or midday outside or in the open. In event of bad weather, indoors will be just as appropriate!.

Set the Altar up in the centre of the Circle so that you face East when working.

The Circle needs to be drawn extra large
The outer edge and the Altar needs to be decorated with flowers, fruit, berries and even vegetables that are in season

The Altar cloth should be white
HP and HPS are dressed in white
The Master of Ceremonies {MOC} whether male or female, is dressed in green

On the Altar are two pillar candles:
A gold pillar candle for the God on the left
A green pillar candle for the Goddess to the right
There is an additional large white pillar candle located on the Altar

A cauldron of water is located to the front of the Altar with a heath aspergillum beside it
Locate a chaplet of Holly {for the Holly King} and one of Oak {for the Oak King} with a folded dark colored shawl, or scarf next to the Altar

Other accessories:
Two taper candles, one for the HP and one for the HPS to light the Quarter candles

Thurible/ censer with charcoal and lighter with Incense
lying beside it, dishes of salt and water, chimes, symbols for
deities {e.g.:shell/ crystal and cone}
Small carafe and bowl of anointing oil, goblet of wine, bowl
of nuts
Libation dish and two pentacles; one larger one and one
smaller one to consecrate the salt located in center of the
Altar
BOS on stand with page weights
The Covens Wands and/ or Athames are placed on the
altar.

Litha – Lesser Sabbat
Summer Solstice

Can contain a Full Moon Rite or New Moon Rite
Insert Rite here if applicable

MOC sounds the Gong three times
With the HP and HPS leading, the Coven moves deosil around the circle,
dancing faster and faster with some playing or improvising on musical
instruments as they wish. HP and HPS start chanting and singing the
Witches' Rune with the Coven joining in,
The Witches' Rune was written by Gerald Gardner and Doreen Valiente for the
Gardnarian Book of Shadows, 1957.

The MOC sounds the gong three times, all slowly halt and the singing of
the Witches' Rune ends with the Call and Response to 'Eko, eko' being
chanted a few times.
Singing bowl sounds 3 times over the chanting, which then dies down.

HP, HPS and MOC stand at the Altar

MOC says:
Litha, longest day
Shortest night holds sway
Golden Sun stands highest in the sky
The turn of Nature's Wheel is nigh

Covener:
The Sun stands at Zenith's peek
Oak and Holly King rival seek

Covener:
The God and Goddess on this day do wed
Fauna, Flora, fertile fed

Covener:

God and Goddess merge as Whole
Union Mind, Body, Soul

Covener:
Litha's pow'r supreme
The Sun from highest point does gleam

Covener:
Mother Earth most fertile being
In great abundance powers freeing

Covener:
Thanks to our Sun Gods solar power
Celebrated at this Litha hour

MOC motions for all to sit while HP and HPS remain standing for the symbolic
enactment of the Marriage.
The HP, HPS and MOC stand at the Altar, MOC with back to Altar, the HP and
HPS facing one another – HPS to MOC's right, HP to his/ her right.
HPS and HP hold hands, MOC lays his/her hand on top of theirs.

The MOC looks to the Sun God; the HP
MOC recites

THE WEDDING OF THE GODS

Power of Life Force
Globe of the Light source
Shining forth to Earth
For Mother Nature to give birth
In union on Litha celebrated
As the Sun God here is venerated

MOC looks at the Goddess/ HPS
Natures infinite soul
And birth giving role
The grand celestial womb

Birth, life, death, rebirth
From cradle to tomb
Around Mother Earth's girth

MOC refers to both:
Here do thee form One
With Mother Earth and the Sun

In unison, the HP and HPS say:
Seed to the Light
Warm and bright
To Mother Nature
Unrivaled stature
Life to Fauna and Flora
Enlightenment in Aura

As the HP and HPS say this, the MOC traces the Invoking Pentagram of the Earth with his/her power hand above the two. The other hand still resting on the HPS and HP's held hands.
The MOC lights the large white pillar candle and holds it between the HP and HPS, over their clasped hands.
MOC:
Let there be light in this Union bright

The HP and HPS hug and kiss
The HPS takes up her Athame and holds it across her chest
The MOC takes up candle and holds it in front of herself/ himself
The HP holds the cauldron/ chalice with both hands before the HPS and MOC.
MOC sings/ recites

AT ZENITH'S PEAK

Great power of Sun and light
Of energies warm and bright
Source of inspiration insight
Cause of germination growth
Sun and Earth here to betroth!

Give us fertility in great abundance
Send all evil to assundence
Give us yielding fields and rivers full
Let us respond to Nature's push and pull
Make us hear Her music sound
And feel Her energies abound
Let us relish in love and life
Banish all evil strife
Let the seed burst forth from Mother Earth's crust
Energies with wholesome thrust
May the union of Fire Water bear the fruit
For all to fully suit
Let us see the light in life's great maze
To in wisdom, insight blaze
Here is to You, our Sun and Earth
Source of Life, rebirth

Symbolic Grand Rite

The MOC traces the invoking Pentagram of the Earth above the Cauldron/
Chalice
The HPS clasps the Athame, point down, in both hands held high and slowly
lowers it to just above the water.

HP and HPS state in unison:

Sun to Earth!
Blade to Cauldron!
Light to Dark!
Seed to Fruit!
Man to Woman!
In love and generation!
In respect and veneration!

HPS lays down the Athame
MOC replaces the candle and takes up the cauldron/ chalice of water from the
HP
HPS takes up the heather aspergillum and sprinkles water over the HP and MOC
HPS recites from

BLESSED SACRED WATERS

Be ye blessed by sacred Waters
Symbol of our Western Quarters
Consecrated Water of life so pure
Blessed, infused by light and Sun
To all evil, banish, cure
By Nature's Wheels yearly run
Substance of the Life Force
Symbol of the Soul's course
Birth, death and renewal
Water, Earth and Sun and fuel

All members of the Coven led by the HP move deosil around the Altar.
As they pass the MOC holding the sacred water, the HPS sprinkles each covener
as they make a wish while being sprinkled and blessed.

The MOC replaces the consecrated water and sounds the gong three times.

Music and song as all dance deosil around the Circle, singing the Choral from

BLESSED SACRED WATERS CHORAL

HP, HPS and MOC lead while groups of Coveners sing the verses in Choral

Choral 1
This is the Sun God's brightest hour
God and Goddess in wedlock flower
Abundance, aplenty in great shower
By Nature's creative power

Choral 2
The Sun God has reached full power
He clothes us in golden shower
His warmth quickens the life force
As the cycle turns, resource

Choral 3

The God and Goddess here conjoin
In wedlock, Sun and Earth for life to coin
As the two form One and All
Earth and Sun, birth to call.

Choral 4

The life sap is rising
The seed is growing, sizing
The shoot is forming fruit
Ever pulsating life blood
In seed, to shoot to bud

Choral 5

Litha, physical and spiritual awakening
In-sight, knowledge, a thirst for slakening
Sun and Light, its highest peak
Sign post for the path we seek

The Crowning of the Holly King

NOTE:
The Concept of the Oak and Holly King as representing the Light and Dark half
of the Year:
By Stewart and Janet Farrar
From: A Witches' Bible, Phoenix Publishing, 1981, 1984
Words by Silver Elder

The Gong is struck three times
All stop dancing. The MOC, HP and HPS stand at the Altar
The HPS nominates two men from the Coven.
She picks up both the Holly and the Oak wreath and waves them over the heads
of the two men kneeling in front of her at the Altar.

HPS says:

Kings of the Waning and Waxing Year
Bringer and taker of the light so clear
Lords of the Fire, ignitor of Nature's pyre

Dispeller of the cold, the season past and old
Usherer of the warmth and light, energy respite

The HPS lowers the Oak crown on one of the two heads and the Holly crown
on the other.
They take up position in the centre of the Circle and dance around the Altar in
mock battle
The Coveners sit around the Circle periphery.
Two Coveners give "commentary" while the "battle" ensues.

Covener:

The Oak King's rule has ended
His power is suspended
The Sun's zenith will descend
Soon day and night shall blend
The Sun will rise further north
And coldness shall pour forth
Over the horizon, the Sun stands lower
Gone will be the season for the reaper, sower

Covener:

The Holly King shall take the throne
From this day on, once reaped what's sown
The ebb and tide is waning
The powers of the God are draining
As the corn ears swell to full
And seeds drop by gravities pull
Spilling forth onto the ground
Ensuring next year's harvest sound.

The Oak King has been "defeated" and lies close to the Western Quarter candle
The Holly King takes off the Oak Kings crown and holds it aloft
A Covener drapes a black or dark veil over the Oak King
Holly King recites the

THE HOLLY KINGS RULE:

Look up!, - for here is the Oak King's crown

The Ruler of the Waxing Year, is down
As the Earth has supplied abundance replete
And winter shall come, oh, so discrete
For in tune with Nature's Wheel
The Season's fate is sure to seal
As the days will grow shorter
And the sun sinks sooner in the Western Quarter

In the next months of six that I will rule
There shall follow this very dual
When the Oak King shall be reborn
To ensure abundant harvest, growth and corn
Until then, it is my turn
The stewardship of the Waning Year to earn
The Sun's brightness shall diminish
And the harvest time shall finish
For respite, all will yearn
The break of Winter all will earn
Energies will slow in the Sun's diminished glow
And the life force shall retreat
In the knowledge that all barns are full, replete

And I shall watch over the lands asleep
As the darkness envelopes by slow and steady creep

The Holly King lays the wreath on the Altar
HPS says:
Such is Nature's ebb and flow
Energies ebb and grow
The Life Force swells and wanes
As our God, in strength and weakness gains
Litha, Nature's climax on the Wheel
Insight, power, energy and feel
And as we all do know
Once we reap what we did sow

182

Nature's forces shall decline
And the sun shall lesser brightly shine
It's the time for introspection
On Litha's lessons learnt
Moral state selection and stripes well earned

HP says
For like our Sun God at Litha's power might
We all do reach the top, to give in to struggle fight
No longer are we center stage
In this material world
But have wizened in spiritual age
And have seen past the Veil unfurled
Such is the lesson of Nature's Wheel
As we spool down the years of our aged real
Let us make the most of Litha's bounty
As we see the riches throughout state and county
For as we pass on the scepter to the younger set
We have been the receptor of our inner divine spark met

MOC says
It's a joyous time and feeling sublime
That through our inner eye
It's insight we espy
For like our Sun God who steps back
Because of physical limit lack
Though keen in mind
He brings light to the inner blind
That knowledge thirst
For that insight burst
He has that feeling nervous
That knowledge veil is pervious
And is keen to know more
And embarks to explore
And by Samhain he knows

With a wisdom that shows

This Rite is followed by Cakes and Wine/Ale
Which is in turn followed by the
Closing of the Rite

Lughnasadh
Greater Sabbat

Northern Hemisphere: 31st July – 1st August
Southern Hemisphere: 31st January – 1st February

Harvest Festival
Lammas
Harvest Home
August Eve
Cornucopia [Strega]
Feast of Bread
Calan Awst

SONGS/ POEMS

First Harvest
On the Silver River Flow

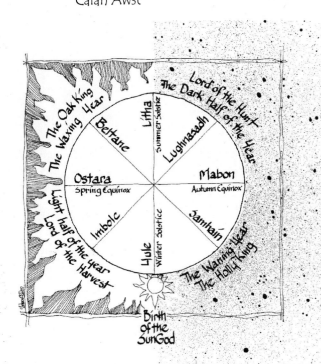

The Altar and Circle

This Sabbat can be held in the evening outside in the open, however indoors is just as appropriate in event of inclement weather!

Set Altar up in center of circle so that you face East when officiating.

The Circle needs to be drawn extra large
The outer edge of the circle and the Altar should be decorated with wheat, rye and/ or corn bushels alternating with apple tree branches bearing fruit, assorted fruit and berries, even vegetables that are in season.

The Altar cloth should be yellow/ orange
HP, HPS and the Master of Ceremonies {MOC}, whether male or female, is dressed in white

On the Altar are two pillar candles:
Gold pillar candle for the God to the left,
Green pillar candle for the Goddess to the right
There is an additional large yellow pillar candle located in a small cauldron, or fire proof vessel, on the Altar
A wheat, rye and corn wreath is located on the Altar.
A dark or black scarf or shawl lies folded beside the Altar.
Each Covener has prepared a two line rhyme about something they wish to give Thanks for in celebration of the First Harvest.

Other accessories:
Two taper candles, one for the HP and one for the HPS to light the Quarter candles

Thurible/ censer with charcoal and lighter with Incense lying beside it, dishes of salt and water, chimes, symbols for deities {e.g.:shell/ crystal and cone}
Small carafe and bowl of anointing oil, goblet of wine, bowl of nuts
Libation dish and two pentacles; one larger one and a smaller one for consecrating the salt located in center of the Altar
BOS on stand with page weights
The Covens Wands and/ or Athames are laid on the Altar.

Lughnasadh – Greater Sabbat
Harvest Festival

NOTE:
The concept of the Sacrificing of the Corn King as symbolizing the Sun Gods diminishing power and strength in relation to the ripening and harvesting of the Corn is based on research done by:
Janet and Stewart Farrar
A Witches' Bible, The Complete Witches' Handbook
Phoenix Publishing, Inc. USA, 1981
Words by Silver Elder

MOC sounds the Gong three times and with the HP and HPS leading, the Coven moves deosil around the Circle, walking or dancing as each sees fit. Some play or improvise on instruments to accompany the singing/ reciting.
HP and HPS start chanting and singing the Witches' Rune with the Coven joining in.
{The Witches' Rune was written by Gerald Gardner and Doreen Valiente for the Gardnarian Book of Shadows, 1957.}

The MOC sounds the gong once and all slowly halt. The singing of the Witches' Rune ends but the Call and Response to 'Eko, eko' is chanted a few times.
Singing bowl sounds 3 times over the chanting, which then dies down

HP, HPS and MOC stand at the Altar
MOC announces:
Behold!, it's Lughnasadh, Greater Sabbat meet
And we our God and Goddess and Corn King greet
It's the harvest of abundance
The celebration of fecundance
It's the Thanks Giving for richest bounty
Throughout the land and county
As the Season's light shall wane
And the life force from the Earth shall drain

HP says:

188

We gaze upon our Corn King's ailing health
His life force drains by stealth
The powers of light and warmth here dissipate
As Winter's onset we anticipate
For we shall reap the ears of standing corn
And the dying life force we shall mourn

HPS says:
But the seed shall fall from this fertile ear
To grow in riches for next year
Such is the cycle of rebirth
Of our greatest Goddess Earth
As Fire and Earth shall join
For new life to coin

Coven Call and Answer
The Refrain of:

FIRST HARVEST

Covener
It's the time of the Waning Year
Winter's nigh, that's clear
The sun stands lower in the sky
The colder months are nigh

A few Coveners sing in scat vocal: Its the Time!...Its the Time!...Its the time!...

Covener
We give thanks for the richest harvest
No one needest starvest
Corn, fruit, rich and full
Crops and stock and wool

A few Coveners sing in scat vocal: Its the Time!...Its the Time!...Its the Time!...

Covener:
In our bounty's Summer, lets rejoice
For plenty range and choice
In strength and power and health
As well as produce wealth

A few Coveners sing in scat vocal: Its the Time!...Its the Time!...Its the Time!...
Others sing in scat vocal: Lets rejoice!...Lets rejoice!...Lets rejoice!
Covener:
It's the time of night sky constellation shift
As towards Winter we adrift
Of a shorter day and cooler night
Migration's birds take flight

A few Coveners sing in scat vocal: Its the Time!...Its the Time!...Its the Time!...
Others sing in choral long drawn out: T'wards Winter we adrift....
Covener:
Heat and warmth rises from the ground
Completion cycle, ripeness does abound
The harvest scythe will sweep
All bounty will it reap

A few Coveners sing in scat vocal: Its the Time!...Its the Time!...Its the Time!...
Most Coveners chant in between the scat vocal: Time!...Time!... Time!...
Time!
All sing in choral long drawn out to the crescendo sound of singing bowls:
T'wards Winter we adrift....

HPS signals for each Covener to pick up a grain bushel lying along the circle edge. The Coveners stand along the circle edge and face inwards.

MOC, HP and HPS stand at the Altar. HP wears the corn wreath.
Coveners start to move slowly deosil, around the circle, holding the bushels
aloft, swaying them from side to side.

The MOC rings the Gong three times
The MOC states:
Birth, death and rebirth
Such is the Law of Earth
Life is finite and manifest
Such powers in our God's invest
The seed of light that awakes the Soul
Such is our divine God's role

The MOC sounds the Gong three times
Birth, Death and rebirth
Such is Life on Earth
Unmanifest, invisible and infinite
Such is our Goddess's Rite
The life giver Soul of Nature
Such is our Goddess's Stature

The MOC sounds the Gong three times
The God's own solar power
Is a'waning at Lughnasadh's hour
As the corn ears seed begins to drop
Signaling the ripeness of the crop
Here comes the harvest time
For the crop that's in its prime

MOC sounds the gong three times
At Harvest time its life sublime
Seed to soil, product of our toil
There to lie and sleep
To grow for next year's reap
By next season sun to be awoken
For the harvest season be bespoken

Nourished by our Goddess Earth
Sowing, growing from birth in girth

HPS says and the Coven repeats while still waving the grain bushels:
Seed to Earth, Cycle Birth
Rain to Land, crops shall stand
Sun and Earth conjoin, new life to coin
Man to Woman cleave, new life conceive

Death of the Corn King

HP bows his head, wearing a wreath of wheat, and slowly sinks to his knees, kneeling.
The Coven is still slowly moving deosil around the circle, swaying the corn bushels.
Covener announces while the HPS lights the large yellow pillar candle in the small cauldron holding it in front of her:
Its nearing harvest's end
Seed to soil shall blend
The Corn King is at peak and prime
The end is coming of his time
It's the climax of his Rule
And the ending of his life's spool

Covener 2:
He has passed on the seed
His life force energy freed
Within Mother Earth's crust
Next Season's life shall thrust

Covener 3:
The Corn King's life is sacrifice
At Lughnasadh's role of dice
Thus marks the Cycle thrice
Waxing, Waning, Price

The HP slowly 'collapses' on the ground
MOC ceremoniously removes his corn wreath
HPS kneels beside him placing the cauldron with the lit candle beside him,
casting light onto his body
Coveners lower their bushels and one by one scatter them around the circle.
One by one, the Coveners drop to their knees around the 'dying' Corn King

The MOC states, sounding the smallest chime once:

The Corn King lies dying
His life 's denying
His seed has been spill't
His energy is wilt
His body material
With Earth is united
His Soul Ethereal
With the Underworld requited

HPS/ Goddess draws the dark veil over his body and snuffs out the candle in the
cauldron

HPS sings from:

ON THE SILVER RIVER FLOW

Rest Ye well on your Underworld Journey
Drifting away on a gossamer gurney
On the Silver River Flow
In the Underworld to blossom, grow

Coveners pick up the apple branches lying around the Circle periphery and hold
them over the Corn King's 'dead' body and the Altar, while walking deosil
around the circle. A Spoked Wheel resembling the Wheel of the Year should
form.
HPS still kneels beside the 'dead' Corn King.

The MOC states/ sings

Slowly, slowly, the Corn King glides
In the Underworld he soon resides
His Soul, his body shall depart
For a new life it soon shall start

MOC sounds the smallest chimes once
HPS says/ sings
Down the river of life Ye go
As all of us do know
Ye shall pass the Underworld gate
To take up the throne and sit in state
And there Ye shall unite
As God and Goddess great
During Winter's cold respite
As She carries your seed inside
As new Season's life 's implied

MOC sounds the smallest singing bowl slowly
Covener 4 says/ sings
Safe journey down the river flow
Under the silver Moon light glow
In the silent quiet water swirl
A new life force shall unfurl
And like the apple branch is bearing fruit
The Goddess Mother Earth, the King shall suit

Covener 5 says/ sings
The Earth, its riches giving
In great abundance living
So She shall need to rest
To recover from Her Quest
And as Lughnasadh's Mabon harvest closes
The Goddess Mother Earth reposes
In the Corn King God's Underworld abode
She carries the new life code

Covener 6 says/ sings
This is the secret of the Apple Isle
It carries the life code phial
The Law of Cycle Threes

An infinite life decrees
As the Goddess carries the life seed womb
And regenerates birth to tomb

Covener 7 says/ sings
Onward down the river flow
As the Wiccan Mysteries know
In the cycle new life'l grow
For as we reap we also sow
Life shall manifest anew
As life force shall accrue
Like the axiom: apple fruit
From seed, to bud, to shoot

Coven Choral Refrain:
Sung in three voices
The Corn King enters the Western Portal
To the realm of life immortal
For like the blade the chalice met
The seed's in place for new life set
And like the Season's wheel is turning
The blue print for renewal is burning
On life's grand plan potential
And everlasting infinite existential.

Once the Singing of the Choral ends and dies down the MOC takes up the
Conga drums/ Bodhrán and softly starts drumming. The Coveners replace the
apple branches along the Circles edge.
Prior to the Sabbat each Covener has prepared a small rhyming note of
something they wish to give thanks for which will now be read or sung as the
Thanks Giving.
The HPS divides the Coven for the singing in multiple voices of the:

THANKS GIVING FOR THE
FIRST HARVEST

Voices 1 starts up and sings in scat vocal: We give Thanks!...We give

Thanks!...We give Thanks!...

Voices 2 follows and sings in scat vocal the repeat: Thanks!...Thanks!...
Thanks!...

One by one each Covener sings/ recites what they wish to give thanks for as the
rest scat in voices 1 and 2

Covener:

...For a life of Plenty; crops and food
by Sacred life force accrued

Voices 1 sings softly in scat vocal during the recitation and boldly on
completion: We give Thanks!...We give Thanks!...We give
Thanks!...

Voices 2 follows and sings in scat vocal the repeat: Thanks!...Thanks!...
Thanks!...

Covener:

...For the Earth that bears
by Season's fecundant cares

Voices 1 in scat vocal, softly during the recitation and boldly on completion:
We give Thanks!...We give Thanks!...We give Thanks!...

Voices 2 follows and sings in scat vocal the repeat: Thanks!...Thanks!...
Thanks!...

Covener:

...For senses that inform
and a life lived by sacred norm

Voices 1 followed by Voices 2, as described above

Covener:

...For all dreams realized
of goals idealized

Voices 1 followed by Voices 2, as described above

Covener:
...For all inspired visions
and considered decisions

Voices 1 followed by Voices 2, as described above

Covener:
...For all acts of kindness
and sympathetic mindness

Voices 1 followed by Voices 2, as described above

Covener:
...For the Fork in the Road
that leads to our sacred abode

Voices 1 followed by Voices 2, as described above

Covener:
...For a life by signal sign
and the Song of the Divine

Voices 1 followed by Voices 2, as described above

Covener:
...For a life of lessons in action
informed by intuitions faction

Voices 1 followed by Voices 2, as described above

Covener:
...For the Sacred way
outlaid each waking day

Voices 1 followed by Voices 2, as described above

Covener:
...For all guidance
and divine presidance

Voices 1 followed by Voices 2, as described above

Covener:
...For each new dawn
and opportunities born

Voices 1 followed by Voices 2, as described above

Covener:
...For that voice primordial
and guidance audial

Voices 1 followed by Voices 2, as described above

Covener:
...For the depth of the Dark
for us to see the Spark

Voices 1 followed by Voices 2, as described above

Covener:
...For the Harvest of bounties wealth
and our Souls integrated health
Voices 1 followed by Voices 2, as described above

Covener:
...For the Sacred story
celebrated at Sabbat's glory

Voices 1 followed by Voices 2, as described above

Covener:
...For compassion
and love received in like fashion

All together as the MOC, HP and HPS 'sing' the singing bowls
'We give Thanks!' long drawn out on 'Thanks'

This Rite is followed by Cakes and Wine/ Ale
Which is in turn followed by the
Closing of the Rite

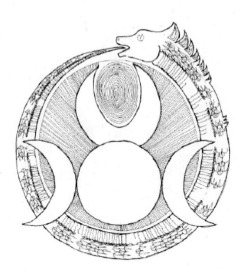

Mabon
Lesser Sabbat

Northern Hemisphere: 23rd September
Southern Hemisphere: 21st March

Autumn Equinox
Second Harvest
Alban Elued - The Light of the Sea

SONGS/ POEMS

Quest for the Goddess
On Mabon's River

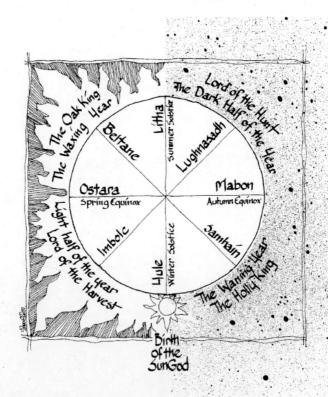

Please consult current astrological diary for the correct dates

The Altar and Circle

This Sabbat is preferably celebrated in the evening, going into sunset outside in the open. Celebrating it indoors in event of bad weather is just as appropriate.

Set altar up in center of Circle so that you face East when officiating.
The Circle needs to be drawn extra large
The outer edge of the Circle and the Altar should be decorated with apple tree branches bearing fruit, assorted fruit, berries and nuts, even vegetables that are in season

The Altar cloth should be rust red or dark brown

On the Altar are two pillar candles:
Gold pillar candle for the God to the left,
Silver pillar candle for the Goddess to the right
An additional red pillar candle in holder should be standing on the Altar
As many white taper candles as there are Coveners.
Each Covener should have a two line rhyming verse about something they wish to give Thanks for during the Second Harvest:- this theme continues on from Lughnasadh's First Harvest.

A folded dark or black veil/ scarf should lie beside the Altar
Coven dressed in customary black, HPS wears a white tabard over her black robe

Other accessories:
Two taper candles, one for the HP and one for the HPS to light the Quarter candles

One additional large red pillar candle
Thurible/ censer with charcoal and lighter with incense
lying alongside it, dishes of salt and water, chimes, symbols
for deities {e.g.:shell/ crystal and cone}
Small carafe and bowl of anointing oil, goblet of wine, bowl
of nuts
Libation dish and two pentacles; one larger and the smaller
one for consecrating the salt should be located in center of
the Altar
BOS on stand with page weights
Sword and boline are optional. Wands and Athame's are
located on the Altar.

Mabon – Lesser Sabbat
Autumn Equinox

MOC sounds the Gong three times and the HP and HPS lead the coven in a deosil direction around the circle, walking or dancing as each sees fit. Some Coveners play or improvise on instruments accompanying the singing/ reciting of the Witches' Rune:
Written by Gerald Gardner and Doreen Valiente for the Gardnarian Book of Shadows, 1957.

The MOC sounds the gong three times and all halt. The singing of the Witches' Rune ends with the Call and Response of 'Eko, eko' being chanted a few times.

HP, HPS and MOC stand at the Altar. The MOC motions Coven to kneel and then announces:

Opening Prayer

Coven kneels on one knee in a circle around the Altar.
HPS is at the altar holding the additional large red pillar candle, already lit, in hand
HPS starts:
The year stands on the edge between space and time
As can be felt by clime
The warmth is draining from the soil
Thermal cyclic recoil
Cold has come to fill the void
With Winter's restful sleep deployed
Days and nights are equidistant light and dark
Though gone is hopeful's summer spark
As t'wards Winter's respite Mabon slides
And Nature's Wheel towards darkness glides
It's the time of balance weighing
As Nature's pendulum is swaying

The end of Summer's toil
The seed lies dormant in the soil
The life force drains away
In equidistant night and day
As energies dissipate
For winter to anticipate

All rise and slowly move deosil around the Circle. HPS returns large red pillar
candle to the Altar
Glockenspiel and singing bowls in different resonance's played by different
Coveners
Gong is struck once, one or two singing bowls continue.

Covener 1:
As Mother Earth its bounty does reclaim
And Nature's Wheel has turned another Season's frame
As the leaves from trees, they fall
The Goddess answers Her Consort's Call

Covener 2:
Our God the Western Portal has entered
And on the Underworld throne is centred
Slain as the Corn King on Lughnasadh's Eve
The Goddess weeps in grief
As by Moon boat he has departed
And o'er the lands the Fall has started

HP says boldly:
Singing bowl crescendo
Though by Blade to Chalice done
New life ensues at Ostara's Sun

Gong strikes once
Covener 3
It's the energy's withdraw'l
In the cycle of recall
As the land prepares to rest

With secret life invest

Covener 4
Year, cycle, season, light is waning
Earthly life force draining
Mother Earth receives what she has gave
Thanks to Yuletide's Sun God knave

HP says while walking deosil around the Circle to stop near the Western Quarter :
It's the Cycle of the One and All
Complete at Mabon's Fall
As we have received
By our Goddess conceived
As the bounties seed that grows
Is now cut by sickle blows...
Though, like water to the Earth
Life's ensured by the seed's rebirth
For like Harvest's seed is now spill't
For regeneration will'd

The HP stops and falls down 'dead' inside the deosil moving Circle near the Western Quarter Candle.
Coven halts and sits down along the Circle edge facing inwards
The Covener closest drapes the black veil over the HP's head
HPS stands at the Eastern Quarter candle, holding the large red pillar candle, already lit, high above her head.

HPS as the Goddess, sings/ recites the

QUEST OF THE GODDESS

It's the balance of light and dark
That signals Mabon's Mark
Night and day are equal
Awaiting Samhain's sequel

Fare Ye well, Lord of the Light Year
Bounty bright, sky, light and air so clear
Germinator of the seed
From cold and ice thus freed
And by the blood of life is formed
Inside my womb, the Earth is warmed

Fare well to Life force
As Nature takes its course
Fare well, King of Corn
As I weep forlorn

Though by Chalice and Blade
The Grand Plan is made
And life shall return once more
The seed shall flourish, which I bore
At Litha's Altar divine
Shall be borne at Yule sublime

Covener sings solo/ recites from THE QUEST or to musical
accompaniment eg: flute, guitar, etc:

Open are the Western Portal gates
As the God our Goddess there awaits
As the land in sleep recovers
God and Goddess, Underworld lovers
Respite from the toil
Rejuvenating soil
A deep and peaceful rest
Preparing for waxing vigor, zest

The HPS, as the Goddess, moves around the Circle 'searching' for the God
She holds the red candle as a light to guide her, while 'searching'

Covener:
The Sun God is at rest
From His waxing year Quest

On the Underworld throne He resides
On His personal quest He presides
Awaiting the Goddess Divine
To let His inner spark shine

Covener:
Looking, searching, seeking
She's heard Her Consort speaking:
Where is the way
To the God's Underworld stay?
Show Her the path
To the Underworld hearth
Where is the throne
Of the God alone?
Show Her the door
The God alone, no more!

Suddenly, the HP, as the slain Sun God, beckons from under his veil
"I am here
So far, yet so near
Bringer of my inner light
Open up my eyes to untold sight
Bearer of the seed, of waxing life decreed...
Find Ye the River Moon boat
Steer by star and float!
Awaiting Ye by safe voyage
Freed from Summers employage
Freely pass the Portal
Closed to lesser mortal
Enter at East, my Rising Moon Queen
Silver light and wisdom unseen!"

HPS lies along side the Altar, head facing West and feet facing East as a Covener
places the red pillar candle in small cauldron on her chest. Coveners gather the
apple tree branches from around the Circle perimeter.
Taper candles are passed around and one by one the Coveners move widdershins

around the HPS, as the Goddess 'resting' by the Altar as they fare well "the Goddess" on Her Underworld journey. As they move past the Altar, they light their tapers from Her red pillar candle in the cauldron.

Coveners hold the apple branches up high to converge in the Altar 'centre' and the HPS acting as the Goddess, while they hold the lit taper candles in the other hand held outward tracing the circle edge. They move in widdershins fashion forming a moving spoked Wheel symbolic of the involving energies prevailing at Mabon.

Covener sings/ recites accompanied by others while other choose to hum:

ON MABON'S RIVER

By the sacred apple bough
A safe passage we wish Ye now
On the Silver River flow
Departing forth we see Ye go
On glittering silver moon light
Primordial and infinite

At the apple fruit signing
Ye, the energy immortal
Shall enter the Eastern Portal
To our God's life aligning

In life and love Ye shall unite
A love unreservedly requite
Enlightening our Sun God's soul
For insight, wisdom, whole

And in the Underworld Ye shall abide
On the throne by our God's own side
His consciousness Ye shall uncover
In Your role as wife and lover

This Grand Union at Samhain takes place
His cerebral sides shall face to face
Blade to Chalice Rite once more

The United Self is the Whole and score!

Coven Choral
of
ON MABON'S RIVER CHORAL

Sung in three voices
Choral 1
Row, row, down the river flow
A gentle silver stream
A glittering glistening gleam
All toil shall cease
Quiet restful peace

Choral 2
Enter through the Eastern gate
Our God to win his fate
The divine spark shall ignite
Depth of knowledge insight

Choral 3
The divine union shall manifest
By the Sun Child at Yule so blessed
The sun again shall rise
It's Nature's Wheels reprise

Choral 4
Our Goddess brings the promise of rebirth
Rejuvenation of the Earth
Bringer of light and insight
The germinator of the seed
From Winter's cold thus freed

The MOC sounds the smallest chimes once. The HPS replaces the red candle in
the cauldron on the Altar and rejoins the Coven. Coveners have replaced their

apple boughs along the Circle edge. They retain their lit taper candles. MOC motions Coven to be divided into a two voice choral for the Voice 1 and Voice 2 scat vocal.

MOC, HP and HPS join Coven in moving widdershins around the Circle, consistent with powers and energies descending or involving similar to the sap that is dropping in deciduous tree causing the annual Fall.

The MOC begins to beat the bodhrán/ conga drums softly.

THANKS GIVING REVISITED
MABON'S SECOND HARVEST

Voices 1 softly starts up and sings in scat vocal: We give Thanks!...We give Thanks!...We give Thanks!...

Voices 2 follows and sings in scat vocal the repeat: Thanks!...Thanks!... Thanks!...

One by one each Covener sings/ recites what they wish to give Thanks for as the rest scat in voices 1 and 2

Covener:
...For a Time of Introspection
and quiet Self Inspection

Voices 1 sings softly in scat vocal during the recitation and boldly on completion: We give Thanks!...We give Thanks!...We give Thanks!...

Voices 2 follows and sings in scat vocal the repeat: Thanks!...Thanks!... Thanks!...

Covener:
...For the deepest dark
past Mabon's mark

Voices 1 followed by Voices 2, as described above

Covener:
...For the Crone's guiding voice
offering wisdom choice

210

Voices 1 followed by Voices 2, as described above

Covener:
...For Dis the Darkest Lord
reconciliation: Light and Dark accord

Voices 1 followed by Voices 2, as described above

Covener:
...For the Hidden
now to the Light is bidden

Voices 1 followed by Voices 2, as described above

Covener:
...For inner secret Grail!
Now it's time to bid ye: 'Hail!'

Voices 1 followed by Voices 2, as described above

Covener:
...For the Grand Descent
and personal growth ascent

Voices 1 followed by Voices 2, as described above

Covener:
...For inner rest and peace
let all action cease
Voices 1 followed by Voices 2, as described above

Covener:
...For Soul and Psyche
and the Union of Light-Dark alike

Voices 1 followed by Voices 2, as described above

Covener:
...For the Night
and rejuvenation's respite

Voices 1 followed by Voices 2, as described above

Covener:
...For my shadow Self side
to embrace instead of hide

Voices 1 followed by Voices 2, as described above

Covener:
...For a time of personal enquiry
and the Shadow's inventory diary

Voices 1 followed by Voices 2, as described above

After all Coveners have given Thanks the MOC signals the Coven to divide up into the Choral/ scat of 'We give Thanks' and 'Thanks- Thanks!' to be sung with gusto for a few rounds before the gong strike signalling
Cakes and Wine

...Which is in turn followed by the
Closing of the Rite

The Esbats

The Esbat Rituals

The actions in this section are common to each of the Esbats.
They are referred to in all Esbat celebrations
as being part of their Rituals
They are:

Preparation
Opening the Rite
Casting the Circle
Calling of the Quarters and Inviting the Deities
Cakes and Wine
Banishing of the Circle and Closing the Rite

The Triple Goddess

Define area of the Ritual
Mark out the Circle on the floor/ ground

Purification of the Circle Area
Sweep designated Circle area with besom

Purification of the self
Bath and wash, dress, focus and relax, visualize and meditate on the coming event, tune in on prevailing energies.

Locate pillar candle of appropriate color at Four Quarter points:
Below is the Southern Hemisphere layout/ reverse for Northern Hemisphere
East – yellow / Air – Elemental Ruler: Paralda
South – green / Earth - Elemental Ruler Ghom or Ghob {North in the Northern Hemisphere}
West – blue / Water - Elemental Ruler: Niksa or Neksa
North – red / Fire - Elemental Ruler: Djin {South in the Northern Hemisphere}

Use your own address or that used by your Coven or Grove for the God and Goddess:
e.g: Lord and Lady, God and Goddess

e.g: "Cernunnos and Aradia, daughter of Diana and Apollo"
Decide on an address for the Quarters:
e.g: Rulers or Kings

Place all tools on the Altar:
2 pillar candles:
The God: Gold, located to the left
The Goddess: Silver, located to the right

{The colors are optional, the candles could also be plain white}
Optional symbols to accompany the candles could be:
e.g: sea shell for the Goddess and a seed cone, horn or stag sculpture for the God.

Plain black Altar cloth however, optional colors according to Moon Phase could be:
Waxing Moon: Light green
Full Moon: silver or black with silver star/ moon print

Waning Moon: Autumn colors of rust reds/ browns
Dark/ New Moon: purple

Two small taper candles for the HP and HPS to light the
Quarter candles
Candle snuffer and lighter
One larger Pentacle to charge or consecrate items in
general and one smaller pentacle to consecrate the Salt,
Athame{s}, Wand{s}, Coven sword, if used
Carafe of anointing oil and small bowl to mix oil and salt
Chalice of water, bowl of salt
Cauldron with/ without candle, if required
Chalice of wine, libation goblet and dish, plate of cakes or
bowl of nuts
Wine, Ale, Mead, Metheglin, Beer or soft drink according
to taste
Small hand bell, chimes, singing bowl or gong, according to
preference
Censer with charcoal and incense
BOS with Ritual on stand with page weights, if the Rite is to
be held outdoors

Set up the Altar:

Locate Altar in the centre of the Circle to face East
Place the pillar candles to the rear: one for the God to the left/ one for the
Goddess to the right, light them
Place the larger Pentacle to the front centre with the smaller one beside it.
Locate Chalice with water and the container with the salt near them. These
would be near the 'Goddess candle'.
Place the BOS with Ritual, on stand, to centre right, close to the Goddess
candle. Ensure page weights when practicing outside.
Two smaller additional taper candles to light the Quarter Candles, lay them
along side the BOS with lighter.
Lay the snuffer alongside the BOS
Place the senser to the left, near the God candle and light the charcoal,
Locate container of incense, charcoal and lighter near it
Place the carafe of anointing oil and bowl of salt to purify, near the Goddess

candle/ to the right of the Altar
Lay the Coven sword, if applicable, across the Altar table between the God and
Goddess candles, to the rear, with all other items in front.
Locate the Athame{s} and/or Wand{s} centre right near the front
Locate chimes/ bell next to Athame{s} and Wand{s},
Position singing bowl, or gong suspended in stand, to the front of the God
candle

Locate Plate of Cakes and Ale, Beer, Wine or soft drinks beside/ under the Altar
if not enough room on it, or, to the left in front of the God Candle.

If the Esbat requires the cauldron or additional pillar candle, this should be
positioned on the Altar to the left.

Other details, which are optional could be a seasonal vase of flowers, cones,
fruit, stones, etc – these could be displayed to the rear, centre between the
God/ Goddess candles

Place all musical instruments/ seasonal items {flowers, corn ears, apple boughs,
etc} to be used in the Esbat along the inside of the Circles edge

If required: CD player/ Hi-Fi running on batteries, should be located near/
below the Altar

Opening Rite

The person designated as the Censerer lights the God and Goddess candles on the Altar. They also light the charcoal in the censer. He/ she does not light the Quarter candles but leaves to join the rest of the Coven waiting outside of the Circle, usually in the souther-eastern quadrant.

The MOC*, HP and HPS stand before the Altar and face East. *{Note: although the title says Master or Maestro of Ceremonies, this person can be either male or female}

With eyes closed they focus and begin to draw down energy from the Cosmos via the crown Chakra and up, from the centre of the Earth via the soles of their feet. They feel the energy converge in their Solar Plexus where they then channel it down their arms and hands and into the tool.

The MOC sounds the gong, chimes or bell three times.

MOC, HP and HPS together say:

"This Rite has begun"

Circle Casting

Note: Depending in whether it is the Waning or Dark half of the year or the Waxing of Light half of the year, the HP or HPS scribes the Circle:

Waning half of the Year: HP

Waxing half of the Year: HPS

The HP or HPS faces East and lifts the tool; Athame or Wand, up to approximately eye level or higher on both hands with open and flat palms, thus presenting the tool.

HP or HPS moves to the Eastern edge of the Circle, holding the Athame or Wand with both hands. He/ she infuses the tool with energy, visualizing a blue-white beam issuing from its tip while holding it pointed at the scribed circle on the ground. He/ she begins walking deosil or sun-wise along the edge scribing the Circle in white light on the ground.

In the Northern Hemisphere, this is East, South, West, North, East {with overlap}

In the Southern Hemisphere, this is East, North, West, South and East {with overlap}

HP or HPS says on return:

It is our/ my* will insight to instill
To cast away blindness by introspection-kindness
In bountiful growth living by Nature's Oath
In the spirit of the Light, honest, good and bright
**I/ we cast this Circle by the powers of the Goddess and
God
Here may they manifest and bless their child*/ children,

*Example of modification for Solitary practice
**Coven name or personal Craft Name here

HP stands at the Altar facing East and presents the chalice of water, holding it in
both hands and raising it to eye level.
He places it on the larger Pentacle. He takes his Athame or Wand, clasping it
between the palms of his hands with point down over the water.

The MOC rings the chimes once

The HP says:
Blessings of the Goddess, infuse this Water
Symbol of renewal, and our Western Quarter

HP scrapes a little salt from the salt dish onto the smaller Pentacle.
He clasps his Athame or wand, point down over the salt on the Pentacle.

The MOC rings the chimes once

The HP says:
Blessings of the Goddess, be upon this Salt, symbol of the
Earth
Mother of Life and the locus of our birth

With the tip of the Athame or Wand, the HP scrapes some of the salt from the
Pentacle into the chalice of water.
He lays the Athame/ Wand aside.
He lifts the chalice with both hands and swirls the water deosil or sun-wise,
three times. He raises the chalice high over the Altar.

HP says:
Water and Earth
Elements of birth
By touch, purify
By power, sanctify

Great Goddess, be You adored

The HP proceeds to walk deosil around the Circle, starting at the Eastern Quarter. As he does so, he sprinkles the scribed Circle edge with consecrated water using an aspergillum made of herbs in season or other seasonal leaves formed into a bunch. Failing this, he uses is fingers.
As he walks, he says:

Water and Earth
Cleanse this Circle girth
Purify and Sanctify!
Cleanse by Waters clear!
Protect by Earth so dear!

On return, he replaces the chalice on the Altar

The HPS takes up her Athame, faces East and presents it.
The HPS presents the burner with the already burning charcoal and places it onto the larger pentacle.
The HPS clasps her Athame, or Wand, in both palms with point down over the burner.
The MOC rings the chimes once

She says:

Blessings of our God, be upon this Charcoal, symbol of Fire
May I/ we achieve my/ our intent to fulfil Your desire

The HPS presents the incense.
She puts a small amount of incense onto the small pentacle.
She clasps her Athame, or Wand, with point down over the incense on the small pentacle
The MOC rings the chimes once

She says:

Blessings of our God, be upon this incense, symbol of Air
May I/ we have your guidance in my/ our soul, intentions fair

HPS lays her Athame aside
She places the incense onto the charcoal in the censer
She raises the burner high over the Altar
HPS says:

Fire and Air

219

Elements so Fair
By touch, purify
By power, sanctify
Great God, be You adored

The HPS proceeds to walk the scribed Circle deosil starting at the Eastern
Quarter carrying the burner, thereby cleansing the air and generating a
protective wall of ether around the Circle edge.

As she walks she says:

Fire and Air
Elements so fair
Seal this Circle sure
By Ether pristine and pure!

Upon returning to the Altar, the HPS replaces the burner.

The Circle is now defined by having been scribed by Athame, or Wand, in step
one. It is also purified by consecrated Water and sealed by consecrated Ether/
smoke, by steps two and three.

LIGHT
It now needs to be illuminated by sacred light, so depending on the waning
or waxing time of the year, either the HP or the HPS carries the Light around
the Circle; in other words, the person who will not be finally consecrating the
Circle carries the Candle around the Circle periphery. They do this in silence,
visualizing how the light infuses the Ether. This person also lights the Quarter
candles, starting with the Eastern Quarter candles, as they go.

CONSECRATING THE CIRCLE
Then the last step is consecrating the Circle: consistent with either the
waning of the waxing year, this is either the HP or the HPS who scribed the
circle initially. They repeat the first step but now they raise a dome of pure
luminescence:
HP or HPS present their Athame or Wand, taking the tool in both hands, he/
she begins at the Eastern Quarter, walking deosil around the Circle edge. In
doing so, he/ she visualizes how the beam of blue white light issuing from the
tool tip rises to form a wall of bright, clear shimmering luminescence. He/ she
sees how on return to the Eastern Quarter, the dome closes at the apex above
the Altar table. He/ she visualizes how the dome reflects its brilliance into the
Circle bathing it in clear warm light for the coming ritual.

On return, the HP or HPS replaces the tool on the Altar

MOC, HPS and HP stand at the Altar facing East
MOC sounds the chimes three times

MOC, HPS and HP say in unison:
Round and round, the power has bound
This Circle tonight in Otherworld light
May no discord enter,
This sacred Circle Centre
For this is my/ our will,

HPS, HP and MOC repeat:
And so mote it be!

HP drops some of the already consecrated salt into the anointing oil and stirs
with finger
HP faces East and presents the anointing oil
He anoints the HPS with the Celtic Cross on forehead: Circle with an equal
armed cross in the centre
As he does so, he says:
In the name of the God and Goddess, I do thee anoint:
{Recite relevant Craft Name here}
As per Divine direction, They do thee appoint
And They bid thee enter
This sacred Circle centre

They salute {embrace and kiss}
HPS anoints the HP in same manner
She says:
In the name of the God and Goddess, I do thee anoint:
{Use relevant Craft Name here}
As per Divine direction, They do thee appoint
And They bid thee enter
This sacred Circle centre

Depending if the MOC is male or female; the HP anoints the female MOC or
the HPS anoints the male MOC

HP and HPS move to the South Eastern side of the Circle where the rest of the Coven is waiting.

Depending on whether it is the waning or waxing time of the year, either the HP or the HPS carries the anointing oil/ Athame or Wand as the one who cast and consecrated the Circle will now be cutting a doorway into the Circle dome of white light.

The HPS/ HP uses the Wand or Athame to 'cut' a doorway into the brilliant white light dome beginning at ground level scribing a doorway arch in a widdershins direction, thereby partially undoing the original casting and consecration of the Circle. He/ she cuts the opening high and wide enough for the Coveners to enter, ending at ground level again.

One by one, each Covener is welcomed and drawn into the Circle with a hand shake.

As they enter, each member is anointed with the Celtic Cross:

Males by the HPS

Females by the HP

HP/ HPS says:

In the name of the God and Goddess, I do thee anoint:

{Use relevant Craft Names here}

As per Divine direction, They do thee appoint
And They bid thee enter
This sacred Circle centre

Upon anointing each Covener is saluted {embraced and kissed}

Once all are welcomed and standing around the Altar, alternating male and female as far as possible, the HP or HPS seals the door way to reinstate the luminescent dome by re-scribing the arch with their Athame or Wand in the same place where it was scribed originally, starting at ground level. He/ she traces the imaginary line of the doorway in the dome, in a deosil direction, thereby redoing and reinstating the original cast and consecrated dome and Circle.

Once this is done and completed, the HP or the HPS sprinkles a little of the anointing oil over the Circle edge while the other scribes the Invoking Pentagram of the Earth above it, thereby fully sealing it.

HP and HPS return to the Altar

The MOC rings the chimes three times

HPS says:

In peace and love may ye gather here
Under Lunar light, so clear

We bid ye hail and welcome!

MOC rings the gong once
All raise their arms in salute position and say in unison:
{Traditional}
This is a time that is not a time
In a place that is not a place
On a day that is not a day
I/ we stand at the threshold between the Worlds
As the Veil of Mystery unfurls
May the Old Ones protect us/ me
Knowing my/ our present, future, history
As I/ we have vowed to hold true to the Craft
and the Old Ways
'Til the end of my/ our Earth days
Now and forever aft

MOC:
Enliven and empower this event
By inspiration heaven sent
I/ we bid Ye enter my/ our Circle task
Awaken the indwelling divine I/we ask
As I/ we set about to celebrate
And give thanks and elevate
The glory of the Sacred and Nature's Ways
Of insight and inspired days

The MOC rings the chimes three times
All say in unison:
Let now the Quarters be saluted and the Gods invited
Give Thanks and celebrate them for love requited

All:
Hail and Welcome

Calling on the Quarters

Below is the Southern Hemisphere rite: starting in the East, then North, then West, then South and returning back to the East
In the Northern Hemisphere the rite would begin at the Eastern Quarter, then South, then West, then North returning back at the Eastern Quarter.

HP and HPS take up a taper candle each, present them at the Altar facing East. They then light them on the God and Goddess candle: The HP lights his on the Goddess candle while the HPS lights hers on the God candle.
Coven faces the direction in which HP and HPS are moving.

EAST

The MOC, remaining at the Altar, gongs the smallest singing bowl once.
The HP and HPS walk deosil to the East.
The HPS lights the yellow candle. Option: Designated Female Covener.
HPS or Female Covener traces the invoking Pentagram of Air above it while saying:

We call upon Air when facing East
And invite You to this spiritual feast
Flight of thought and speed of mind
Thank You for all thoughts kind
As we ask for that mental spark
To action what we hark
Visualizations are appearing
Color yellow golden
Deeds to You beholden
Please attend our Rite, this sacred Esbat night
And guard this Circle with Your might

Coven say facing East:
Calling Air from the East
Enjoy our Spiritual feast

NORTH

The MOC gongs the smallest singing bowl once
The HPS and HP walk deosil to the North or, to the South in the Northern
Hemisphere/ See the words for SOUTH
The HPS or designated Female Covener lights the red candle
HPS or designated Female Covener traces the invoking Pentagram of Fire above
it while saying:

When facing North, we call upon Fire
Rulers of stamina, vision and desire
Thank You for manifest-aspire
And by the color red so bright
Ruler of Spirit and Psychic sight
And the bodies force requite
By the symbol of our Wand
We ask You to respond
Please attend our Right, this sacred Esbat night
And guard this Circle site
Against all evil slight

Coven say facing North:
Facing North, inviting Fire
Stimulate our vision and desire

WEST

The MOC sounds the edge of the smallest singing bowl once
The HP and HPS go to the West.
The HP or a designated Male Covener lights the blue candle
The HP or Male Covener traces the invoking Pentagram of Water above it.

HP or Male Covener says:
We call upon Water when facing West
And bid You enter our Circle, our behest
Rivers, lakes and waterfalls
Rainy misty clouds and drizzle palls
Seat of feelings and emotions deep

In love our hearts do steep
And by the color blue
We come and ask of You
Please attend our Rite, this sacred Esbat night
and guard this Circle locus
From all evil focus

Coven say while facing West:
Calling Water, facing West
Enter our Circle, our behest

SOUTH

The MOC sounds the smallest singing bowl once
The HP and HPS go to the South or, to the North in the Northern
Hemisphere/ See the words for NORTH.
The HP or a designated Male Covener lights the green candle
HP or the Male Covener traces the invoking Pentagram of the Earth above it
while saying:
When facing South, we call upon Earth
Locus of our Rite, home of life and mirth
Stable, solid, pure
A base reliable and sure
We ask You for fibre muscle power
To action the required hour
By the color green or black
We welcome You here back
Please witness this Rite, this Esbat night
And guard this Circle space
From all falsehood and about-face

Coven say while facing South:
Facing South and calling Earth
Come and join us in mirth

Blessing the Quarters

MOC remains at the Altar and sounds the gong three times
HP and HPS walk deosil and arrive back at the East
They raise their arms in Salute

Coven copies their movements and all say:

I/ we seek our Gods' might and power of thought
By wisdom wrought

MOC sounds the gong three times
HP and HPS go to the North/ The South in the Northern Hemisphere - see
words below

All face north, salute and say:

I/ we seek our Gods' might and power of spiritual Fire,
Good intent and the souls desire

MOC sounds the gong three times
HP and HPS go to the West

All face west, salute and say:

I/ we seek our Goddess' power of healing and love
Of empathy and feelings from around-above

MOC sounds the gong three times
HP and HPS go to the South/ The North in the Northern Hemisphere- see
words above

All face south, raise their arms in salute and all say:

I/ we seek our Goddess' power of stability
Of equilibrium and health agility

Casting of the Circle is concluded

The main Esbat Rite follows now after the
Casting of the Circle and the Invoking of the Quarters.

The main Esbat Rite precedes the
Cakes and Wine/ Juice/ Ale and the Closing of the Rite
which comes at the end.

Cakes and Wine/ Juice/ Ale/ Mead/ Beer

{Soft drinks are just as appropriate, should alcohol be an issue!}
SEE PAGE 98 FOR MORE DETAIL
The MOC sounds the gong three times
The person detailed to fill the Altar wine goblet with wine has done so.
The HP, facing East, presents the filled goblet with both hands holding it high above the Altar
He turns to face the HPS holding the goblet in front of her.
The HPS presents the tool; Athame or Wand. Clasping the tool in both her palms, she holds the tip over the wine.

HPS:
By Chalice and Blade
Bless all creation made
By Water to Earth
Bless the locus of our Birth
By Air to Fire
Here's to growth inspire!

HPS replaces her Athame/ Wand on the Altar and takes the goblet from the HP.
HP presents his Athame/ Wand first, then scribes the Pentagram of the Earth above it.

HP:
Let bounty grow by what we sow
Let love infuse this land
Wrought by sacred hand

HPS takes the goblet and replaces it on the Altar

The MOC sounds the gong three times
The HP takes up the plate of Cakes, facing East and presents it with both hands.
He holds it in front of the HPS
The HPS presents her tool; Athame or Wand and then clasps it with both hands to lower the tip over the cakes.

HPS says:

228

Grains, Yeasts, Fruits and Wine
Most blessed and Divine
Fed by Fire, Water, Air
Grown of the Earth with care
We give our Thanks to Thee

All:
And Blessed Be!

The HPS replaces her tool and takes the plate of cakes/ biscuits from the HP.
The MOC sounds the chimes once
The HP faces East and presents his Athame/ Wand and proceeds to draw the
invoking Pentagram of the Earth over the plate.
As he does so, he says:
Lets give thanks and share
And spare a thought and care
For the Gods we love
And Their blessings from above

The MOC sounds the chimes once
Both the HP and HPS now face East at the Altar. The HP holds up the plate of
cakes/ biscuits while the HPS holds up the goblet of wine.
In unison they say:
To the Old Ones
Wise Ones of past Days
Rulers of the Old Ways
In peace we come, in love we part
Insight we sum, as is our Art

The MOC sounds the chimes once

All:
To the Old Ones
Wise Ones of past Days
Rulers of the Old Ways

The HPS takes a cake and breaks off a piece crumbling it between her fingers
letting the crumbs fall onto the earth if the Rite is held outside. If it is not held

outside, she places the piece on a libation dish ready on the Altar.
She keeps the remaining piece for herself and passes the plate on to make its
round around the Circle where everyone takes a cake/ biscuit.
The HP pours a little wine onto the ground if the Rite takes place outside. If
not, he pours a little wine into the libation goblet standing on the Altar before
passing the wine goblet around the Circle for all to have a sip.
Once the plate of cakes and the goblet arrive back at the Altar, the MOC, HP
and HPS eat and drink last.

At this stage, any other foods that may be stored covered under the Altar can
be brought into the Circle to be enjoyed as part of the Ritual. This is a time of
relaxation, enjoyment and sharing of experiences.

Closing of the Rite

The Thanking and bidding the Quarters farewell is done in a widdershins
manner; in an anti-sunwise manner as the energy now involves and the Circle
is closed and cleared. Therefore in the Southern Hemisphere, the Southern
Quarter is fare-welled first, then the West, the North and the East.
In the Northern Hemisphere the Northern Quarter is fare-welled first, then the
West, then the South and the East.
In the same manner, each Quarters is fare-welled by using the banishing
Pentagram of that Quarter/ Element.

The MOC sounds the gong three times.
Coveners all present their tools; their Athames or Wands facing East, then stand
ready holding them in their power hands.

HPS details a coven member to accompany her to extinguish the candle flames

SOUTH
North in the Northern Hemisphere
HP, HPS and Covener go to the South
The MOC sounds the chimes once
Coven turns to face South
HP says, while designated Male Covener traces the banishing Pentagram of the
Earth above the Green/ black candle:

Rulers of the South
All those ruled by the Element of Earth
Symbol of the Five-Point Star
Infinite, divine

The symbol of our Craft, here and far
Earthly, stable grounding
Reliable all rounding
I/ we bid You peacefully depart
And hope to see You soon
By next Ritual Moon

Coven faces South and repeats all movements made by the HP and Male
Covener

All:
Hail and Farewell!
Ave atque vale!

The designated Covener snuffs out the green or black South candle

WEST
HP, HPS and Covener go to the West
The MOC sounds the chimes once
Coven turns to face West
HP says while a designated Male Covener traces the banishing Pentagram of
Water above the blue candle:

Rulers of the West
All those ruled by the Element of Water
Necksa – Ruler Queen
Spirit subconscious, profound unseen
Symbol of the chalice containing water blue
Healing, feeling true
I/ we bid You peacefully depart
And hope to see You soon
By next Ritual Moon

Coven faces West and repeats all movements made by the HP and the Male
Covener

All:
Hail and Farewell!
Ave atque vale!

The designated Covener snuffs out the blue West candle

NORTH
South in the Northern Hemisphere
HPS, HP and Covener go to the North
The MOC sounds the chimes once
Coven turns to face north
HPS says, while a designated Female Covener traces the banishing Pentagram of
Fire above the red candle:

Rulers of the North
All those ruled by the Element of Fire
Symbolized by Sword and Athame
Star, Sun, physical energy
Power guided and directed
Changes are expected
Ruled by Djin, the Ruler- King
Willpower is a-practicing
At the color red
Love and passion said
I/ we bid You peacefully depart
And hope to see You soon
By next Ritual Moon

Coven faces north and repeats all movements made by the HPS and the Female
Covener
All:
Hail and Farewell
Ave atque vale!

Designated Covener snuffs out the red North candle

EAST
HPS, HP and Covener with snuffer, go to the East.
MOC sounds the chimes
Coven turns to face East
HPS says while a designated Female Covener traces the banishing Pentagram of
the Air over the yellow candle:
Rulers of the East
Inspiration, vision, mental
Ruled by Air, Elemental
With Paralda, Ruler – King

Speed of mind and psychic hearing
Governor of herbal wisdom, plant growth
Harmony, truth and personal oath
Ruled by symbol Wand
Mental harmony respond
I/ we bid You peacefully depart
Hope to see You soon
By next Ritual moon

Coveners face East and repeat all movements made by the HPS and the Female

Covener

All say:

Hail and Farewell!
Ave atque vale!

The designated Covener snuffs out the yellow East candle

MOC, HP and HPS return to the Altar and replace tools. The Coven replaces
tools on Altar
The MOC strikes the gong once and motions Coven to sit down.
All do and spend a few moments in silence, grounding energies before the
MOC rings the smallest chime and the HPS starts the choral.

The Coven join in:

Earth, Star and silver moonlight
I am presiding/ We are gathered here tonight
To serve this Esbat Rite
Rulers of the Sun and Moon
Thank You for Your boon
And we/ I hope to see You soon
Guiding light
In the brightest day
And darkest night
You show the way
Wisdom, empathy and love
Streaming all around- above
Fairies, Spirits, Elementals, All
Positive energies You enthral

Purest beauty, deepest love and kind intent
Essence of the Craft as sent
Warming feelings do abound
Good will flowing all around

Repeat Choral:
By Chalice, Wand and Athame
May we/ I always work in harmony
Blessed be!
Blessed be!
{Some continue singing in scat: Blessed be! Blessed be! Blessed be! –until fade
out}

Entire Coven sings in repeat Choral until fade out:
We sing this Rune
Under the silver Moon
Merry meet and merry part
Blessed be our sacred Art
Merry meet again
Blessed be
Blessed be!

CLEARING THE CIRCLE

In a similar manner as the Quarters were fare-welled in a widdershins direction,
so the Circle will be cleared in a widdershins manner, as the power and energy is
being drawn in, grounded and cleared.
Depending on whether it is the Light or Waxing half of the year or the Dark half
or the Waning half of the year, the HP or the HPS clears the Circle:
Light half of year: HPS,
Dark half of year: HP

MOC sounds the smallest chimes three times.

HP or HPS stand at the Altar and present tool; raising it up on open flat palms
to eye level or higher.
HP or HPS take the Athame or Wand in both hands and walk widdershins to
the Southern Quarter {in the Southern Hemisphere/ Northern Quarter in
the Northern Hemisphere} He/ she points the tool at the luminous line of

the scribed Circle rising from the ground forming the dome. Here, he/ she visualizes how an invisible force beam issues forth from the tip of the tool dispersing the light energy as he/ she moves along the Circle edge; the Circle dome disintegrating with its light dissipating back into the darkness. He/ she moves widdershins from the South to the West, to the North and the East opening and clearing the Circle boundary and the dome.
In the Northern Hemisphere he/ she would be walking widdershins from the North to the West, on to the South, to the East and back to the North.

HP or HPS arrive back at the South before returning to the Altar.
The MOC sounds the Gong three times

The HP, HPS and MOC say in unison:
This Circle is cut!
May its blessings long remain
May we its kindness, love and essence long retain
Merry meet and merry part
Blessed be our sacred Art

All with some singing in scat vocal:
Merry meet and merry part again
Blessed be
Blessed be!

All repeat:
Blessed Be!

MOC strikes the gong three times and states:

This Rite is Ended

HP snuffs the Goddess candle, the HPS the God candle

The Esbat Meditations

First Quarter ~ Waxing Moon

Light

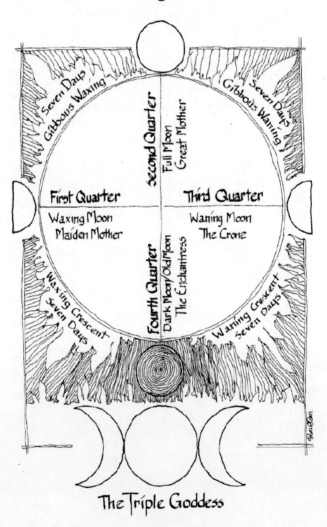

The Triple Goddess

ESBAT

Waxing Moon – Light

Esbat Statement

The MOC sounds the gong three times
All Coveners stand around the Altar facing East. The HP and HPS side by side,
facing Coven
HP leads the introduction of the Rite.

HP says:
Let's honour the meeting between the Maiden-Mother-
Crone
For in our quest we're not alone
And as Nature's wheel continues turning
We grow with continued learning
Corresponding waning, waxing moon phase
From darkness fullness moon blaze
Its growing powers dispel our psychic haze
It's the aspects of the Goddess meeting
As Hekate and Diana 'r greeting
Equidistant interplay of dark and light
A balanced power play in Magick's sight
We gather here to meditate and celebrate
Nature's ebb and tide
And its effect upon the Cosmos wide
The ebb and tide within our psyche
The highs and lows of mental spike
As the Moon phase passes the midway mark
Towards Full Moon we embark

Some Coveners start humming in the background

First Covener says

As Nature's push and pull
Between Dark Moon and the Full
We stand in between
A half Moon is seen
As energy grows
Spirits' message flows

Second Covener says

Some Coveners are still humming while one or two start drumming softly

It's a wondrous time
This evolving clime
As the Moon waxes and wanes
And the Energy grows and drains
We live at Nature's pace
With the God and Goddess, face to face

Third Covener says

Soft humming and drumming continues

With ebb and tide the powers grow
Stronger psychic flow
As light increases
Slowness ceases
As our mind's eye
Forges that ethereal tie
With Spirit connect
The Channel direct

HPS says:

Some Coveners softly scat vocal key concepts while others hum

Light, life essence of Spirit Quintessence
Light, the shining power at our Esbat hour
Whether by Moon, or Sun
By light our work is done
Light guides our heart and mind

For all acts kind
It is by light that we love
And feel guidance all around-above
Light by Spirit and fire
Allows us wisdom to acquire
Spirit and fire on Pentagrams' Star
Infuses us in light to take us far
It is light we take to our Underworld being
To open our hearts and minds all seeing
All negatives transmute
as Light renders to good repute
It is by the light of the Lune
That we sing the Witches' Rune
By the light of our Circle round
We harken for the sacred sound
And see the Deities' sign
With Their message all a-shine

Coven Call and Answer

The MOC sounds the gong once
Coveners start walking and dancing deosil around the Circle as the chosen ones
respond to the statements made.

HPS starts:
Light, the wisdom seed
The essence of the Creed
Light the opening eye
All evil to deny

Covener 1
Light, a positive feeling
Kind thoughts appealing
A supporting task
No need to ask

Humming starts up with scat vocal: 'Light, Light, Light at key breaks in

background.
Recorder or pan pipes/ other wind instrument and soft drumming

HP says:
Light, guidance divine
By deed, event or sign
Light, auric white
A message bright

Covener 2
Light, says, 'I know!'
In confident glow
Light, of pure heart
A bold start

Covener 3
Light, the days' sunrise
Light, goal of the wise
The divine reprise
The Universe comprise

Covener 4
Light, the guided walk
The informed talk
Confident, aware
Light says, 'I care!'

Covener 5
Light, the channeled will
Sacred task fulfill
Light in the mission
Of a sacred decision

Thanks Giving and Prayer

MOC sounds the gong as HPS rings the largest singing bowl. The dancing and
singing fades out as coven kneels around the Altar.
HPS leads in prayer.
The HP and HPS kneel side by side, facing East.
HP leads the introduction of the Rite and Thanks Giving

HPS says:
We give thanks for each task given
To conclusion driven
And the emotions of grace
On a delighted happy face
We give thanks to Nature's forces
That conduct our action courses
By the will of Deity
That we live a life satiety
We give thanks for all data
That we glean from Universes strata
Which allows us the spark
To illuminate the dark
We give thanks for good thought forms
That weather our storms
And acts of kindness
That banish the blindness
The quickened heartbeat
That delights at the feat
The tear in the eye
That says Spirit is nigh
We give thanks for actions directed
By God and Goddess protected
By will on higher planes
Giving us our lesson gains

One or two minutes of silence follow in which all give thanks to the God and
Goddess for their blessings.
The MOC sounds the gong three times

241

Request

Coven remains kneeling
HP and HPS recite the Request together.
So let us turn the page
And furthermore engage
In our quest for learning and light
That we appreciate requite
Open the forest glade
And show us the path outlaid
That takes us on the road
To our ancestral history abode!
Let us see all instances,
Actions, lessons, inferences
To guidance numinous
In sun and moon light luminous
And we shall feel vindicated
By the guidance as indicated!
It is our life to pursue
Experience to accrue
By Spirits presidance
And our God and Goddess guidance

Coven Choral

The MOC sounds the gong as HP and HPS sound the singing bowls. HPS
motions Coven to start dancing. Improvised music starts up on the Chant of
"Ignite the Spark' starting off the Choral
All rise and start dancing deosil/ sun wards around the circle enjoying the
singing in repeat choral, Chant and Choral in Three Part Harmony

Coven Choral 1
Half of the Coven chant 'Ignite the Spark' in background, as other half sing the
Choral:
Ignite the spark
Of love and light

Burn away the dark
By sacred sight

Coven Choral 2
Half of the Coven chant 'Enter all Divine' in background, as other half sing the
Choral
Enter all Divine
Glow in auric splendor
Let the Spirit shine
In wisdom render

Coven Choral 3
Half of the Coven chant 'Infuse us to the deep' in background, as other half
sing the Choral
By moonlight's silver sweep
Infuse us to the deep
By loving tender flow
Of Spirits sacred glow

Coven Choral 4
Half of the Coven chant 'in Love and Joy and Grace' in background, as other
half sing the Choral
Cast away to drift
Evil causing rift
Spirit to replace
In love and joy and grace

Entire Coven sings in Three Part Harmony:
Interplay of dark and light
Power play in Magicks' sight
As we see that Half Moon sphere
Towards the Full Moon we do steer

The MOC sounds the Gong three times and singing/ chanting stops
Dancing and drumming continues
HPS calls out:
Luna, Luna

Coven replies:
Hekata!

HPS calls out
Luna, Luna

Coven replies:
Diana!

HPS calls out
Luna, Luna

All together chant
Aradia!

Spontaneous call and answer continues
{Add as many names as you can think of!}

The HP and HPS return to the Altar where the MOC sounds the largest singing
bowl three times
All focus on the God and Goddess and cast their eyes inward, calming down for
the meditation.
MOC motions Coveners to lie down on their backs around the Altar, crowns
of their heads facing the Altar, feet facing the circle edge. All hold hands. The
smallest chimes are rung three times.
HPS and HP remain at the Altar to lead in the meditation
HP says as HPS sounds a singing bowl softly:
Whirring stirring energy pull
In seven days the Moon is Full
As we see the half sphere
Towards Full Moon we do steer
A cosine line between the energies
Towards Full Moon more power frees
As halfway Hekate and Selene shake hands
Pivotal power flows across the lands
As the Goddess aspect evolves Selene
Etheric powers are less serene

Lune's ever growing draw
In seven days we'll marvel in all awe
As the psychic cup fills up to the brim
And we'll glimpse across it's rim
Into Otherworld realms and quarters
We'll call upon Air, Fire, Earth and Waters

MEDITATION

HP, HPS and MOC share verses while sing bowls sound quietly throughout the meditation.

HPS starts and leads
Let the light come streaming
Like the strengthening first ray beaming
Let it melt away the dark
Leaving only shadow's mark
See this happen in your Underworld
Past the veil unfurled
As you bring the insight
To the darkened blight
Feel your mood lift and the sadness shift
Feel an elation
By the insight revelation
See the sun rise higher over horizons line
As you claim a quest that's won as: "Mine!"

HP says:
Such is our task
As the Deities ask
For they are our inner sun rise
They are our inner moon wise
For we harbour both
By sacred pact and oath
The day and the night
As golden silver light

For they complement each other
Like sister-brother

HPS says:
See the turning wheel of the year
With the cycle change at Yule and Litha clear
This cycle of waxing and waning
Light gaining and draining
By Season's ebb and flow
And sun for crops to grow
Such is our God and Goddess' story
Steeped in Season's light and glory
As light they both dispense
In mutual recompense
And the Wheel keeps turning
As the sun dims and brightens
By Yule's fire burning,
Till Litha's sun heightens

HP says:
Oh, splendorous auric light show
Indicates all psychic know
About a person's state of health
All about their mental wealth
The state of their psyche
And energy spike
With each color meaning
There is knowledge gleaning

HPS says:
Oh, white light dazzling shimmer
A myriad stars a'glimmer
White light us envelopes
As the psychic line develops
As the deities us protect

As harm they may detect
For like our Circle cast
Protects us from the evil blast
Like a white light dome,
Our Outerworld home
As all Magick meets
Where we enact our sacred feats

HP says:
Come hither to the light
And spiritual learning bright
Sweep away all ignorant limitations
And poor sacred imitations
Feel secure
In the Deities' white light pure
Cast all harm asunder
And dismiss all previous blunder
Live in the here and now
And open the third eye brow
And extend your reach
Beyond the earthly breach
Toward the outer stations
And inter-stellar cations
Feel energies contract expand
Through every muscle, tendon, gland
Sense the ions tingle
As with entities you mingle
Open your mind, heart and every pore
To hear the Universal score
Enjoy and love the entities nigh
As you come travel by
Feel the power of light surround
As you explore the Astral profound
As Spirit ever beckons
And the Universe it ever reckons

Know that you are safe from harm
By the God and Goddess white light charm

HPS says:
The Universe is ever extending
With energies ever expending
For us to tap
Into our own cosmology map
As we navigate the route
Our visit to suit
As the God and Goddess know
And in clues us show
We transcend the mundane so crass
To forge ahead in Universe's mass
At light speed and by sacred need
We shall arrive
Divinely alive

HP says:
Our task safely handed
To a soul greatly expanded
So we bring light to dark
To feel that inner spark
By exploring the unknown
As by Spirit shown
For our God and Goddess shall never shy
To show us why
Its for our sacred good
That learn we should

The smallest chimes sound three times
The smallest singing bowl is sung as Coveners slowly return from the
meditation, focusing on its peace and quiet.
HPS bows her head, closes her eyes and spends a moment or two in silence
HP draws the Pentagram of Earth above the HPS's head, lays Athame on the
Altar.

Motion repeated by HPS for HP.

Closing Choral

MOC motions Coven to sit in relaxed position as the HPS leads in song to ground residual energies.
Coven splits up into groups to sing the verses in repeat choral. Some improvise musical accompaniment.

HPS:
Dear Mystery Mother Moon
Thank You for Your boon
Take us on Your course
Infuse us with Your force
Lead us to Your vision source
Here insight to impart
For a new emboldened start
As light meets dark
There is a vision spark

Choral
And the Cycle turns
Lune's glow brightly burns
Here's to Lune gaining
By Cycles' refraining
And Lune appears
As darkness clears

Fade out refrain:
And Lune appears
As darkness clears
The Cycle turns
And Lune's glow burns
Light meets dark
For a vision spark

Repeat refrain
For we honour Thee
So mote it be!

After several chorals sung the MOC rings the Gong three times
to signal the Cakes and Wine Rite

This Esbat Rite is now followed by the Cakes and Wine
which in turn is followed by the Closing Rite

The Esbat Meditations

Second Quarter ~ Full Moon

Time

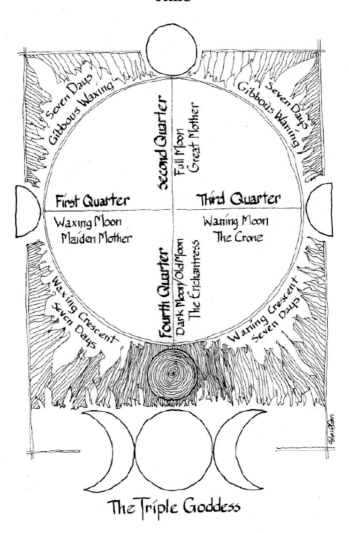

The Triple Goddess

ESBAT

Full Moon – Time

Esbat Statement

The HPS and HP stand at the Altar facing one another with heads bowed and
holding their Athames across their chests.
The MOC stands at the Altar facing East and in between the HP and HPS
Coveners stand around the Circle.
MOC rings the gong three times, then picks up a pillar candle, already lit and
holds in between the HP and HPS

MOC introduces
Once more we meet
At Ghom's soul we seat
Beneath the glowing sky
At Full Moon bright and nigh
Let us pause and think
About our God and Goddess link
Goddess of the Twenty Eight Cycle days
Goddess of mystic fate and ways
Who allows the birds to return from migration's journ
Who makes the crops grow that we decide to sow
Who by governed time makes Season's clime
Who by seven days phases, shines by our Sun God's blazes
Who governs water's tides by ebb and flow
And time abides by Nature's know
Such is the power of Lune
Our Great Goddess Full Moon

One or more Coveners play soft pan pipe music in background
HPS says

252

Great Goddess Mother, we celebrate You here this night
At our Esbat Full Moon Rite
Let us feel Your hand
As You sweep across the land
Bathed in mystic crystal light
Energy source of insight
Let us celebrate in mirth, upon this Earth
Beneath Your silver sphere
With intentions good sincere
Let us celebrate in love
Through Your powers from above
Let us feel Your guidance
Beneath Your stately presidance
Make us the channels
Of Your wisdoms' annals
Connect the line to the power Thine
Make us the conduit
Of Your visionary pursuit
Allow us evil to cure
In actions sure
By Your vision pure
Give us the confidence and stability
By Your psychic agility
To read the scene of life's great screen
Allow us to steer the course
By Your visionary resource
Facilitate the connection to the outer planes
To make the detection for psychic gains
Allow us to hear the cosmic gavel
On quests of astral travel
As decisions are made
By the powers of Your sword and blade
And answers are given
And courses driven
By the outer forces that dictate the courses

By Spirits guidance and Your Divine presidance
Allow us to feel
The statements to reel
Through Universes vibration
And material dissemination
Allowing us to know
By Your inner spiritual glow

Option:
The Rite of Drawing Down the Moon, Page 304 followed by the Charge of
the Goddess; the Great Mother Charge on Page 312 could be enacted here, if
desired and appropriate.

Coven Call and Answer

MOC sounds the chimes three times and motions Coven to sit down within the
Circle.
Tools and candle are replaced on the Altar and the pan-pipes quieten down.
HPS motions the first Covener to start:

First Covener says
Great Mother in Your aspect Trine
At the Waning, Waxing, Full Moon sign
Mother of fulfillment and perfection
Of visionary instillment and selection
Mother of life and birth
Of learning and mirth
Ruler of the Cauldron and the Well
Who makes the seed to fall and swell

Second Covener says
The Moon our Goddess aspect Thrice
Ruler of Fate, the roll of the dice
Lady of the Beasts and of Harvest feasts
Mother, the Life giver
By birth deliver

Third Covener says:

Lady of the Light and insight bright
Lady of Enlightenment,
Hers by entitlement
Lady of Regeneration
As Mother veneration

Forth Covener says:
Lady of Transformation and renewal
As seen from Earth's great Jewel
Waxing, Full and Waning, Dark
Energy pull and draining spark

Fifth Covener says:
Mother of Mystery and many a'history
Ruler of rebirth
At Lune's waxing girth
Mother of principles hidden
By many initiate bidden

HP sounds the gong once

Thanks Giving

The MOC motions the Coven to kneel in semi circle around the Altar
The MOC, HPS and HP stand at the Altar
HPS leads in prayer
Let us give Thanks for a Time free zone
Where our insight is fed and grown
Like a spiritual nursery
Of love and kindness, sans adversary
Let us give Thanks for the ability
To transcend Time with such agility
To breach the threshold
By divine guidance bold
Let us give Thanks to put Time on hold

255

To hear the sacred message told
The whispering in the wind and waves
Like angelic written music staves
Let us give Thanks for the Outer Domain
Where we can insight obtain
Let us give Thanks to Mother Nature Teacher
Who provides us the answers as asked
To quests divinely tasked
With many a learning feature

Three to four minutes of silence follow in which all give thanks to the God and
Goddess for blessings
The Chimes are rung three times by MOC

Prayer and Request

Entire Coven remains kneeling
HP states the Request:
Let our psychic flower
Blossom at any hour
As our deities dictate
And our insight shall equate
To Their will and reason
No matter Time or season
Let our inner Sun's ray
Brighten our cerebral day
Let our psychic water clear
Pour forth any time of year
Let our love and light
Issue any time, day or night
Let our compassionate boon
Sing like a sacred Rune

The MOC rings the gong three times

Coven Choral

The HPS motions for all to rise and begin dancing deosil around the Circle.
Most sing while others improvise music on instruments, eg: Flute, guitar,
ukulele, cow bells, conga drums, etc
Coven is split up into three 'singing groups'

Refrain sung in three voices 1

In love and life combine
By the Goddess aspect Trine
In mirth we celebrate
Our God and Goddess venerate

Refrain sung in three voices 2

Hear the Cosmic Tune
At each Full Moon
Feel the Sun's First Ray
To energise the day

Refrain sung in three voices 3

Feel the powers pour
From the Earthly core
Merging like a river flow
With the solar energy glow

Still dancing, the Coven sings as one unified choir

Coven Choral 1

Solid as a rock ticks Nature's clock
Its own Time-Space measure
At Nature's pace and leisure

Coven Choral 2

Hear angelic incantations
Through all celestial stations
Feel the energies pure
In love and goodness, sure

Coven Choral 3
Listen to the rustle of the leaves
On Mabon's colder breeze
A message Spirit sends
On our action it depends

Coven Choral 4
Liquid silver Lune light
Thank you for love requite
By our Goddess grace
Across all time and space

Coven Choral 5
God and Goddess binary
Oracle source divinery
By Sun-Moon power
At our Esbat hour

Coven Choral 6
By tides' rising and falling
Hear Spirit is a'calling
In the ebb and flow
Of Sun-Moon glow

Coven Choral 7
It's a wondrous world
Beyond the veil unfurled
Of sacred light
And divine insight

Coven Choral 8
It's sensory knowing
By divine sign showing
Through Nature's forces

And her Cycle's courses

Coven Choral 9
Feel the vision on the air
That says, "We know! – We care!"
"We'll show and We'll be there!"

Coven Chant

MOC returns to the Altar as the rest of the Coven dance which turns into the
Chant as the HPS chants Luna, Luna…
MOC beats the largest singing bowl once after each 'Luna, Luna…' to which the
Coven replies in unison, raising arms in salute to each chant by the HPS

MOC strikes the largest singing bowl once
HPS chants
Luna, Luna!

Coven chants
Gaia!

Repeat for all Goddess' names and many others not listed here
HPS: Luna, Luna! – Coven responds: Aradia!
HPS: Luna, Luna! – Coven responds: Gaia!
HPS: Luna, Luna! – Coven responds: Selena!
Coven responds with as many names of Great Mother Goddesses they can think
of: Demetra, Hesta, Vesta, Innana, Hera…even ones that do not rhyme….Isis…
The MOC returns to the Altar and the Gong sounds three times and the
chanting fades out.
There is a moments silence

MEDITATION

The HP, HPS return to the Altar and sound a series of singing bowls as the rest
of the coven stand around the Altar. The MOC motions Coveners to lie down
on their backs around the Altar, crowns of their heads facing the Altar, feet
facing the circle edge. All hold hands.
The HP rings the smallest chimes three times.

259

HPS and HP remain at the Altar to lead the meditation
HPS starts and leads

Time began from nothing, nill
Universe empty, void and still
In a second fraction
Began the action
Thirteen Billion years ago, scientists do know
With energy pure
Came the Time issue cure
From nothing it grew
Time did ensue
Matter won the test
In the Cosmic quest:
Energy as the smallest ball had made the call:
"Let there be the Biggest Bang! –
The Grandest Universal clang!"
Thus the Universe came to being
As today we're seeing
Such was Time's dawning
And its paradigms' spawning
And energies' signal of the first second
As the Big Bang beckoned
Can still be heard by measurements incurred
Testimony to the Creation
Of this Grand Universal Station
This was Time's birth
With Sun, Moon and our Earth
Since then Time is calibrated
Numerated and evaluated
Each and every action
By year, by hour, minute, second, fraction
Time gives meaning
By judgment, mental screening
Time sets the pace
In every realm and place

A creation by us humans
By our own cerebral lumens
Time is a concept only Earth bound
Irrelevant in Universe's realms around
Man uses Time to measure
All of life and pleasure
Time defined by senses, visual and audial
Since time primordial
Therefore time is sensory
A tool from sciences dispensary
Time is our being definition
Our identities disposition
And Time's evolution
Masters the human revolution
It calibrates our day
What we do and what we say
It's the action link
To what we think
Time rules! -
Our norms it schools...

HP says:

Time calibrates change in all life's range
Summer, Autumn, Winter, Spring
Seasonal beginning
Sun's first rays
Heralds in the days
The moon welcomes the night
Day has run its flight
The days, the years are passing
As age is thereby classing
Time as a circle infinite
No end in sight
Time as a linear line
No end define
Though it had a start

With the Big Bang part
As a cosmic place and date
Marked Time's fate
We like to define, expose
As all of science knows
For as long as it has a label
We feel content and stable
So Time's events have names
Set in calibrated frames
By days, weeks and years
Our daily life its steers
Time gives weight
To our efficiency state
Time shall evaluate
Our fate to destinate

HPS says:
Time rules Mother Nature
In all her grandest stature
Through birth, life, death and rebirth
It runs its sadness-mirth
The Cycle it generates
By definition it venerates
From Seed, to Bud, to Shoot – are Time's stages
The Cycle through the ages
Ostara's life burst, Mabon's Fall
All measured by Time's clinical call

HP says:
While Time dictates duty
It can not evaluate beauty
At what hour shall there be the sweet scented flower?
Qualities that transcend Time
Are values higher and sublime
The beauty of what we learn

Timeless as we quest and yearn
Our Spiritual experience
Within the outer realms ethereance
Growth in our minds
Any life stage finds
Free of Time's restrictive binds
A kind thought-form projected
How can Time dissect it
Our journey's on outer planes – not to be inspected
Our dreams meaning
Its symbols gleaning
Our magickal ventures
Free from Time's deep censures:
'In a Place, that is not a Place'
'At a Time that is not a Time'
is what we say in our magick Circle round
free of Earth's Time bound

HPS says:
There are realms transcendental
Of Earthly Time instrumental
Where Time and Scale distort
By Earthly standards wrought
Astral bi-location
Free from Time's dictation
Inner experience and growth
Free of Time's measuring oath
Love, beauty and compassion
Free of Time's limiting fashion

HP says:
As Spirit calls
Earthly Time-Scale stalls
As the psychic channel beckons
Time here no more reckons

For the angelic flower
Opens at any hour
And the vision ray
Shines at any day
And you could be anointed
At any year appointed
For energies transcend
The Earthly Time Scale blend

HPS says:
The higher Spiritual quest
Is free of Time's invest
As the higher Angelic powers
Dispel all Time's office hours
The Call of the inner Voice
Ignores the Day-night choice
And the angelic recital sings
By its own timeless rings

HP says:
The guiding Forces shall decide
When it chooses to preside
For you to action Their will
And Time shall stand still

HPS says:
Such is life on the Outer Dimension
Free of Time's dictates declension
For you are the tool
In the cosmic energy pool
In powers steeped
And abilities heaped
Outside of Time's control
And norms as a whole
You are part of the Otherworld reaches

Beyond Earth's limited breaches
The realms of Energy forces
And different Time-Scale courses
A concept difficult to comprehend
Within Time's limited extent

End of Rite Choral

A few minutes of silence as Coveners ground themselves and enjoy the residual
energy of the meditation
The MOC sounds the smallest chimes three times

HPS, HP and MOC bow their heads and close their eyes in a few moments of
silence. The MOC draws the invoking Pentagram of the Earth above the heads
of the HP and HPS.
Coveners spend moments in silence before ending in a quiet closing choral
Entire Coven sits up in relaxed position after the few moments silence before
the HPS leads in song.
Coven splits up into groups to sing the verses in repeat choral. Some improvise
musical accompaniment.

HPS:
Under Moon and Sacred Star
Calling Energies from near and far
Let us celebrate and sing
Rejoice in our special gathering
Let us feel Your hand sweep the land
Let us celebrate in mirth, upon this Earth
Let us feel Your guidance and constant presidance
Let us be the channels
Of Your wisdoms' annals
Let us be the conduit
Of Your visionary pursuit
Let us celebrate our Lady and Lord
By Athame, Wand and Sword
For we honour Thee
So mote it be!

Repeat refrain
Let us celebrate and sing
At our special gathering
To darkness bring light
Energy bright
For we honour Thee
So mote it be!

Fade out refrain:
For we honour Thee
So mote it be!

After several chorales sung the MOC rings the Gong three times
to signal the Cakes and Wine Rite

The Cakes and Wine are followed by the Closing Rite

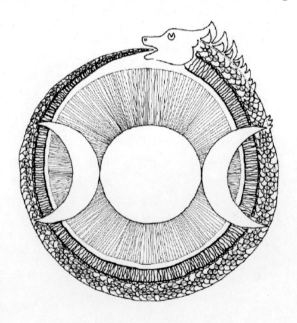

The Esbat Meditations

Third Quarter ~ Waning Moon

Many Chambered House

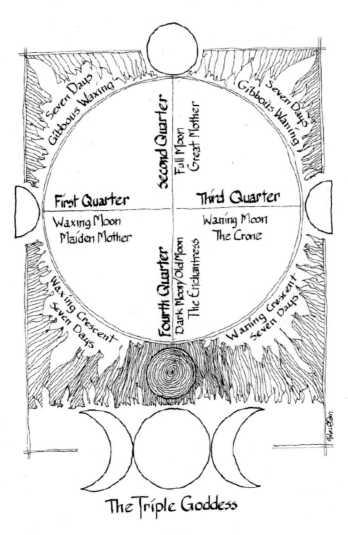

Seven Days Gibbous Waxing

Seven Days Gibbous Waning

Second Quarter

Full Moon Great Mother

First Quarter

Waxing Moon Maiden Mother

Third Quarter

Waning Moon The Crone

Fourth Quarter

Dark Moon/Old Moon The Enchantress

Waxing Crescent Seven Days

Waning Crescent Seven Days

The Triple Goddess

ESBAT

Waning Moon:
Many Chambered House

Coven Call and Answer

The MOC sounds the gong three times and motions the Coven to stand in a
semi-circle around the Altar, facing East.
The MOC, HP and HPS, each holding a candle, stand at the Altar facing the
Coven.
HPS takes the lead in the Coven Call and Answer. Individual Coveners reply.

HPS says and raises candle up high:
Once more we meet
At Ghom's souls seat
Beneath the ever darkening sky
As the moon wanes ever shy

The MOC rings the smallest chime once
First Covener says
Time for us to introspect
Thoughts to gather and collect
Energies, away they seep
Into calmness as we steep

The MOC rings the smallest chime once
Second Covener says
A time of growing peace
Impulses flow and cease
The light grows dimmer

268

The moon grows slimmer

The MOC rings the smallest chime once
Third Covener says:
Welcome the break
A stroll to take
Explore the structure of our mind
Which we deny, ignorant and blind

The MOC rings the smallest chime once
Forth Covener says:
We stand at the evolution of two phases
Draining power, psychic hazes
Betwixt full and new
The ebbing light gives us the clue
A perfect half moon in the sky
Its light the sun will soon deny

The MOC rings the chimes three times
HP steps forward, raises candle high and says:
It's the midway mark
Between light and dark
Power is draining
The moon is waning
Lets take up Hekate's offer
Accept the key that She'll proffer
To hear Her speak
On the guidance that we seek

HPS , HP and MOC state in unison, all raising candles high:
Our Lord and Lady of Their wisdom share
If we our wish to learn declare
Freely of their knowledge They'll impart
To empower us to make the start

The MOC, HP and HPS replace the candles on the Altar

The MOC motions the Coven to kneel and sounds the gong three times

Prayer

HPS leads in prayer
HPS says
As Mother Selene matures to Hekate Crone
Third aspect Divine and shown
As Full Moon wanes
And the light force drains
Hekate's Underworld beckons
As man on Earth here reckons
And Selene grows to Hekate's role,
So do we in Soul
Through integration - recognition
A path in life transition

So, let Hekate turn the key
In Goddess aspect Three
Enter! - Wisdom's Light
By Hekate's learning Rite!

Coven Choral

MOC sounds the gong several times with fade out and motions Coven to rise
and start dancing deosil around the Circle.
HP and HPS join in as the HPS leads in the Choral
Most Coveners sing with some playing/ improvising on instruments such as
banjos, mouth organs, small drums, rattles, etc.
Coven sings in three voices

Coven Choral 1
Some Coveners sing scat vocal: 'The Midway mark, The midway
mark...'
The midway mark
'Tween light and dark
Power's draining

The Moon's waning

Coven Choral 2
Some Coveners sing scat vocal: 'Growing peace, Growing peace…'
Growing peace
Powers flow and cease
Light grows dimmer
The moon grows slimmer

Coven Choral 3
Some Coveners sing scat vocal: 'away they seep, seep, away they
seep, seep…'
Energies, away they seep
Into calmness as we steep
We welcome the break
A stroll to take
Across the divide
To the Otherworld side

MOC sounds the gong once
The dancing stops and singing fades but the drumming continues signalling
beginning of each word/ name
All remain standing as HPS begins the Chant:
Half the Coven chant
Luna, Luna, Hekata!
The other half of the Coven chant
Luna, Luna, Selena!
All together chant
Luna, Luna, Aradia!
Chant continues with as many Goddess names as Coven can think of.

The Gong sounds three times and the chanting stops

Thanks Giving and Request

HP, HPS and MOC move to the Altar while the MOC motions Coven to sit

271

comfortably
HPS steps forward towards the seated Coven with heads bowed
HPS leads:

We wish to thank our Lord and Lady pure
For all that makes us feel secure
Although we have another favour
Our Otherworld to savor
Please show us the path and gate
That leads to that Otherworld state
The path to our Self so real
For us so Whole to feel

HPS steps back to Altar and the HP steps forward

HP:

We call upon our Quarters
Air, Fire, Earth and Mighty Waters
For fluidity of thought
For the Gods' clues sought
For that spark ignite
And psychic insight
For strength
To go the extra length
For all emotions welling
Their content telling
To purify our mind, body and heart
To practice our divine art

HP and HPS take up their Athames and the MOC motions Coven to rise and
stand
HP walks to the Eastern Quarter, then the Southern Quarter
HPS to the Western Quarter, then the Northern Quarter
They stand facing outwards

EAST:
The HP goes to the East, raises his Athame in salute and says:

Coven faces East and repeats the HP's salute
Clear Ether all around
Transparent life force does abound
Breathe through our spirit sphere
Blow away impurities unclear
We order evil to depart and leave
For love divine receive

NORTH

The HPS goes to the North, raises her Athame in salute and says:
Coven faces North and repeats the HPS's salute
Bubbling glowing lava flow
Passion of the heart that's in the know
Excite, ignite, admire
Quell all evil on your funeral pyre
We order evil to depart and leave
For love divine receive

WEST:

The HPS goes to the West, raises her Athame in salute and says:
Coven faces West and repeats the HPS's salute
Unblock the fountain of our soul
To reach our deep emotive goal
Gurgling swirling water clear
Wash away anxieties fear
We order evil to depart and leave
For love divine receive

SOUTH

The HP goes to the South, raises his Athame in salute and says:
Coven faces South and repeats the HP's salute
Blood and bone
Our body's rock and stone
Give us the strength in tendon muscle
And fibre, cell corpuscle

We order evil to depart and leave
For love divine receive

The HP and HPS return to the Altar
The HP and HPS kiss their Athame blades and hold them on their hearts before
laying them down
MOC rings the gong three times.

MEDITATION

HP and HPS stand either side of the MOC who asks the Coveners to lie down
on their backs around the Altar, crowns of their heads facing the Altar, feet
facing the circle edge. All hold hands

HP introduces:
For now we'll focus on our dwelling
Its treasure store of symbols welling
Its attic, basement within our head
That place which people like to dread
It is a most exciting venue
With an age old menu
As old as we can walk erect
Aged symbols there detect
So let us open the door
With Hekate's key
And walk the floor
To learn and see

HPS starts and leads
As we look upon ourselves, our hair is turning grey
We stare at the mirror, there we say
We're growing senile, decrepit, fragile, old...
But then we feel a hand grabbing hold:
"Sister!, Brother!, you have an infinite resource
Of unrestricted recourse...
Experience, wisdom, insight

274

Always there, day or night, joy or plight
Access to the seventh dimension
With spiritual extension
Achieved by life time learning
And spiritual quest and yearning
With the God and Goddess coming to your aid
To help, direct and keep you stayed!"

HP says:
We have glimpsed across Daath's Divide
And feel our hearts swell with pride
We have walked many chambered houses
And responded to queries this arouses
We have crossed many a river flow
Arriving on the banks, enlightened- in the know
Climbed and sat on many a mountain top
And harvested many a knowledge crop
Some have lived a life full throttle
Through a haze of sad emotional mottle
And we have had our hand on the tiller
Through stormy seas and winter chiller
And have guided the vessel to life's great berth...
Steering the ship through uncharted waters
But thanks to our Divine and Spiritual Quarters
We are berthed stable and sound here on Earth!

HPS says:
As we explore this house room by room
We could very well assume
We've learnt a lesson or two
As we have muddled through
Its earthly span and life's grand plan
With lessons to be applied
In the next life other side
But our earthly life is not over yet

275

And its end date is not set
For the Gods have drunk a toast
To our new appointed post
For this is to impart and teach
And extend our reach
To all those who dare to knock
Regardless of life's passage clock...
It's us who stand beside the door
With Goddess' help to set the score
For all who wish to enter
Into the Spiritual center
Of life's multi-chambered house
Where Hekate holds the key
And provides the light to see
Across the divide to the other side
Into each cranny and nook
As we turn the pages of our own book
And as our story here evolves
Many a life saga here resolves
For we begin to realize, in sum and size
That the house addressed
Is our Underworld repressed

HP says:
Dreams and symbols, stories draw
Us through the Underworld maw
Here we look explore
And walk the secret caverns
Lives lived in Underworld taverns
The wondrous world of our own history
By Hekate's key to our own mystery
A real and living part
With symbols that inform our heart
It's the other half of our brain
Quiet, functional and sane

HPS says:

It's our many chambered dwelling
As nightly symbols are upwelling
Part of us like life and limb
Available fit and trim

HP says:

An infinite facility to integrate
A tool our daily life to impregnate
A resource we do not wish to loose
It's available for daily use

HPS says:

For us who live and love our Craft
It's the key from which to draft
Empathy, love and deep compassion
To help others in right fashion
As we have made the journey inward
We can direct assistance kin-ward
As we have walked this path before them
With our Gods as we adore them
To help, direct, prepare
As through insight we're aware

HP says:

Through introspection it's knowledge that we glean
As we walk this dwelling's room with treasures yet unseen
Making us an integrated soul
In heart, mind and body whole.

End of Rite Choral

A few minutes of silence as Coveners enjoy the peaceful energy of the
meditation
The MOC sounds the smallest chimes three times

HPS, HP and MOC bow their heads and close their eyes in a few moments of silence. The MOC draws the invoking Pentagram of the Earth above the heads of the HP and HPS.
All tools are replaced on the Altar. Coveners spend moments in silence before ending in a quiet closing choral to ground residual energy.

Entire Coven sits up in relaxed position after the few moments silence before the HPS leads in song.
Coven splits up into groups to sing the verses in repeat choral. Some improvise musical accompaniment.

HPS:
Let go, let flow, release
Relish in the peace
Feel sadness drain
With hope to gain
Time for evil to vanish
Pain to banish

Choral

Background scat vocal: let go, let flow, release, relish in the peace
A new course is drawn
Under the waning dawn
And darkness sweeps around
Envelopes all on earthly ground
As the forces dissipate
For the new start anticipate

Fade out refrain:
A new course is drawn
Under the waning dawn
Forces dissipate
For new start anticipate
To darkness bring light
Energy bright
For we honour Thee

So mote it be!

Repeat refrain
For we honour Thee
So mote it be!

After several chorales sung the MOC rings the Gong three times
to signal the Cakes and Wine Rite

The Cakes and Wine are followed by the Closing Rite

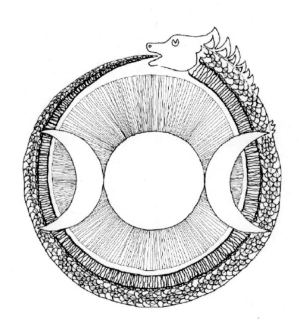

The Esbat Meditations

Fourth Quarter ~ Dark Moon

Manifestation

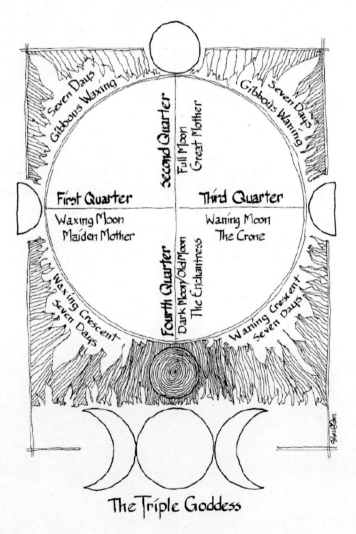

The Triple Goddess

ESBAT
Dark Moon – Manifestation

Thanks Giving

For Dark Moon Esbats all Coveners are given a candle in a holder as they enter
the Circle, after the Welcome. Female Coveners light their candle on the HP's
candle, while male Coveners light theirs on that of the HPS.
HP, HPS and MOC stand at the Altar facing the Coven
The MOC strikes the gong three times and motions Coven to kneel in a semi-
circle around the Altar facing east
All hold their candles and ponder the light in the time of deepest darkness

HP says
Once more we meet again
In our meadow clearing forest glen
With our Lord and Lady to commune
And meditate upon the Witches' Rune
And this night as the moon is new
And no energy is likely to ensue
We cast our eye inside our heart
And await our Gods' advice impart
Upon a new direction start

HPS
We also wish to Thank our Lord and Lady
For being part of the chosen few
Who seek the essence and the clue
Who are given the tool
By the divine inspired school
To follow our calling
Officiating with enthralling

281

To practice at the divine Altar
By guidance so we shall not falter

MOC
We give thanks for such love and kinship
Of the cosmic family we are a part
As we feel in soul and heart

MOC strikes the gong three times and motions Coven to rise and stand
The HPS, HP and MOC stand at the Altar facing the Coven standing equidistant
around the Circle perimeter

Coven Call and Answer

HP leads, stepping forward and holding candle
Nominated Coveners step forward in turn and recite their verse
HP
We thank our Gods for their guidance
For their patience and presidance
For we know we're not alone
But protected, never evil prone

First Covener says
Our Lord and Lady also know
The secrets that we never show
This includes our deepest needs
Advice and actions for future deeds

Second Covener says
Our Lord and Lady know what we need to learn
The inner knowledge for which we yearn
Insight which we wish to gain
Access to that higher plane

Third Covener says
Tonight we meditate upon our life stage

Our life's direction, path and age
The wish for greater expertise and skill
Our Craft more fully to fulfil

HP says
Our Lord and Lady of their wisdom share
If we our wish to learn declare
Freely of their knowledge they impart
And empower us to make the start

Three to four minutes of silence follow in which all give thanks to the God and
Goddess for their blessings or make a request for help

Coven Choral

The MOC sounds the gong three times and motions Coven to assemble in a
semi-circle in front of the Altar. All are holding their candles. HP, HPS and
MOC stand at the Altar facing the Coven. The MOC breaks the Coven up
into two groups to sing the Choral in two part choral with some playing or
improvising on musical instruments.
HP and HPS lead the Coven in the Choral.
HPS leads Choral 1
HP leads Choral 2

Choral 1 lead by HPS starts:
Here is to our God and Goddess' host
And their street sign post
To show the way
And as we stray
To guide us along
Through life's bustle throng

Choral 2 lead by HP
Here is to a heart unblemished
With love replenished
For our Gods' own will
Our mission to fulfill

Prayer and Request

MOC strikes the gong once as the singing fades
HPS motions the Coven to kneel. All still hold their candles

HPS says:

We give thanks for our Craft that we so enjoy
And healing powers we can deploy
As we focus and project
Our destination we select
We visually see and create
What we hope will emanate
To then ethereally precipitate
The concept seen deep inside
Through powers that within us reside
Thus we have abilities to heal
To empathize and feel
And cast the appropriate spell
To help others get better and well

HPS

However there we have a request to ask
If you could please help us in our quest and task
About the Laws of Congruity we wish to learn
A deeper insight to gain and yearn

MOC

We meet and here remind
Our fellow Craftly kind
Of these infinite laws
And our moral mores
And the results of any abuses
From any wrongful Ritual uses

Three to four minutes of silence follow as all consider their situation in life and
on this Dark Moon Esbat night.

The Gong is rung three times

Coven Choral

The HPS motions Coven to walk deosil around the Altar to return candles.
MOC breaks Coven up into three groups to sing the Choral in three part
harmony with some playing or improvising music.
Once all candles are returned to the Altar, the HP and HPS lead the Coven in
dance and Choral.
HPS leads Choral 1
HP leads Choral 2
MOC leads Choral 3

Coven Choral 1
We introspect
On cause and effect
On ethereal vibration
Giving form animation

Coven Choral 2
Our willed-forms scatter
Within the cosmic matter
As thought-forms we send
Earthly bounds transcend

Coven Choral 3
And on cosmic levels they resound
Having escaped all earthly bounds
And in this way our spells transcend
To manifest at destination's end

All in Unison
We're part of a greater whole
In mind and body, soul
Cosmos never ending
Life and death transcending
Earth and spirit blending
Though-forms are a'sending

On waves ethereal
To become matter material

Coven Chant

MOC sounds the Gong three times. The dancing and singing slowly fade out
and stop. The Coven are motioned to file past the Altar to pick up their candles
with all males lighting theirs on the Goddess candle and all females lighting
theirs on the God candle. They stand randomly around the Circle. MOC, HP
and HPS stand at the Altar, holding their candles
MOC gongs the largest singing bowl

HPS steps forward, raises candle high and chants:
Luna, Luna!
Coven raises candles high and chants:
Liliya!
MOC gongs the largest singing bowl

HP steps forward, hold candle high in the air and chants
Luna!, Luna!
Coven holds candles high and chants
Aradia!
MOC gongs the largest singing bowl

HP and HPS both step forward holding candles aloft
Luna!, Luna!
All chant in unison, holding candles high
Hekata!

MEDITATION

The MOC rings the chimes three times and motions Coven to place their
candles equidistant around the Circle edge.
HPS motions Coven to lie down on their backs in a circle/ star formation with
their heads facing the Altar and their feet facing the Circle edge. All hold hands.
MOC, HP and HPS remain at the Altar
MOC rings the smallest singing bowl

HPS starts and leads
It's a special feeling
To sense the powers correspond and reeling

As they manifest within the chosen locus
Via visualization focus
As they pass along the cosmic vibration
To the appointed destination
And the thought and will transcend
To arrive at destination's end
It's the wondrous sight to see the will take route
And manifest as we wished to suit
These are the skills within us latent
Which we can develop to make more patent
Abilities we wish to hone
Via advice from Hekate, Crone

HP says
For this is our will and so mote it be
We often say, decree
And after having enacted and spoken
In deed, words and token
Our will at the Altar
Willing that it shall not falter

HPS says:
But what happens next we ask
To manifest our required task
As our warm breaths dissipate
On another level to coagulate
In vast space-time
To maybe manifest in another place and clime
For like Ouroboros, the dragon swallowing its tail
The time, space, action cycle will never fail

HP says:
As the Moon phase
Waxes and wanes through Time's haze
And as Nature's cycle annually turns

Moon sets, sun rises as the light burns
So in a time space continuum do we live
And through death new life we give

HPS says:
We consider here, the Kabbala Tree
Explaining the phases of reality
For the Divine Will and the All
Exist throughout the Cosmos's pall
Our will is created in Kether's glow
Our idea as seed to sow
It is in our mind that we create
And through air and inspiration activate
The archetypal concept takes on shape
As from Kether's realms it moves, escape
By sacred Lightening Bolt
To in future arrive at Malkuth, with a halt

HP says:
Through Briah our idea takes form
By cognition it takes norm
And by will and action ruled by Fire
Into realization turns our desire
As we set about with hands to make
Our idea for shape to take
Passing through Yetzirah's world
The formation realm, consciously unfurled
Here, by many virtues our idea 's infused
By qualities of power and splendor, with splendor used
And by divine Will, reality to instill
As its essence further evolves
To manifest in Malkuth, there resolves
Thus is the ever happening now and here
Life on Earth as we see, feel, smell and hear

HPS says:
What we need to comprehend
As our consciousness extend
It is the Law of Syncronicity and its effect
As through actions done, responses we'll detect
For our thoughts, words and deeds
On Etheric planes a response there breeds
As by vibrations through matter concepts resonate
To in different time-space zones reactivate
For what we give we shall receive
For how we live, is how we ideas conceive

HP says:
This is Congruity in Law
What we do, returns for sure
As actions dissipate in essence
In atoms, matter, ether, effervescent
In sympathy to resonate
And returns to us, reciprocate

HPS says:
For here we are part of a greater whole
As we sense and know within our soul
And energy flows on vibration's wave
For us information to glean and save
Its how we concepts send, emit
On healing spells set free, transmit
In positive vibrations there to resonate
And within the recipient to activate
This is how thoughts and visualizations we do project
The manifestation of Cause and Effect

HP says:
It's a love of life on Higher Planes
A linking into cosmic concept trains

That puts us in tune
With energy flows from Lune
It's that silver cord bind
To our divine kind
That cosmic link
With which we feel and think

HPS says:
That ability to listen deeply
Into ether we're ascended steeply
As we feel the waves concealed
To us honestly revealed
As we visualize all detail
Of the future without fail
As we penetrate nebulous layers
Of all those expert truth sayers
To expose the core
Of all falsehood lore

HP says:
By our Creed we are bound
To positive energy resound
To ethically do our best
Such should be our quest
To use these powers
Infusing us at Esbat hours
To transmit help where needed
And give advice where heeded
We have these powers deep inside
And by our Rede we must abide

End of Rite Choral

A few minutes of silence as Coveners ground themselves and enjoy the residual

energy of the meditation
The MOC sounds the smallest chimes three times
HPS, HP and MOC bow their heads and close their eyes in a few moments of
silence. The MOC draws the invoking Pentagram of the Earth above the heads
of the HP and HPS.

Entire Coven sits up in relaxed position after the few moments silence before
the HPS leads the quiet End of Rite Choral sung in multiple voices as the Coven
is split up into groups to sing the verses in repeat choral.
Some improvise musical accompaniment.

HPS:

In the deepest dark
Resides the spark
Of New Moon light
And vision bright

Choral 1

It's the season of Hekate Crone
Of Spirits' reason by insight sown

Choral 2

Young and fresh, inspired
First light so admired
Your faintest crescent
Silver, iridescent
Returned from the dark
To ignite the cosmic spark

Choral 3

Shine on us Your light so fine
Infuse us with Your wisdom, thine
Lune, always recurring
As we keep discerning
An unending refrain
With insight to gain
In ever growing lumen
Divine in ancient numen

Choral 4
The Cycle shall turn
The Sun shall burn
To make the Moon to shine
New, Quarter, Full and fine
To light up the sky
As Luna-Selena nigh

Choral 5
So rest in the Ebb and Flow
And the Lunar Cycles Ebb and Grow

Repeat refrain
By Wand and Sword and Athame
We honour Thee
So mote it be!

We honour Thee
So mote it be!

The MOC sounds the gong seven times

The Cakes and Wine Rite is followed by the Closing Rite

The Esbats

Drawing Down The Moon

The Charge of the Goddess as related to
the Moon Phase:

The Maiden ~ Mother Charge
The Great Mother Charge
The Crone Charge
The Charge of the Enchantress

Moon Phases and Correspondences

First Quarter	Second Quarter	Third Quarter	Fourth Quarter
Waxing Moon	Full Moon	Waning Moon	Dark Moon
Maiden ~ Mother	Great Mother	Crone	Enchantress

The Esbats are dictated by the Moon phase indicating a specific aspect of the Goddess generating certain energy flows; involving waning powers conducive to introspective spells and personal growth on an internal level or the evolving waxing energy of the active conscious extrovert persona. The Esbats are commonly held at night, preferably in the open where the Moon is visible at all Quarter stages except one, the Fourth Quarter; the Dark Moon. They are ideal opportunities to generate group energies for the enactment of Magick as well as generating powers conducive to Channeling.

Furthermore, the Esbats celebrate the Moon as the symbol of the sacred feminine and hence feminine energies as symbolized by the Goddess. This, in no ways diminishes the role the Sun plays in making manifest the Moon in the night sky by its reflected light. In fact, it is the ultimate manifestation of the binary nature of the relationship between the God and Goddess as complementary to one another. The Sun and Moon act as symbols of these juxtaposing energies and powers that exalt the masculine and feminine in all forms of life to make life manifest in Nature that forms the core of Esbat celebrations. Hence, the Sun and Moon become analogous to psychological processes taking place within our own Self; our Soul. We therefore 'read' the story of Nature being the story of the God and Goddess, to heal ourselves and grow as reconciled and integrated beings.

The Moon phase and its energies become synonymous with our own life cycle, the life cycle of the day, the life cycle of the year making up the Laws of Nature of which the Moon is the most compelling symbol forming the central focus of the Esbats.

'The Charge' as a written piece of Pagan liturgy gives physical form and experience to the key Pagan concept that the Divine is immanent and can be revealed and celebrated within us all. In combination with meaningful Ritual, this experience is profound, leading to an enhanced sense of mystery and increased perception by all senses thereby unlocking the latent potential within us to perform Magick and divination such as Channeling.

294

Thus the Rite of 'Drawing Down the Moon' and 'The Charge' are sacred statements of desired Spiritual outcomes sought in Paganism, namely the awakening of the indwelling divine. It is enacted at most Esbats, especially at Full Moon Esbats, whereby the Goddess is invoked by the High Priest within the High Priestess. Once the Goddess and the High Priestess are perceived to be fully integrated and acting as a single divine entity, the Goddess speaks through the High Priestess in the form of 'The Charge' and 'uses' the High Priestess as a vehicle and a channel. If the Rite is properly conducted and the required altered state of mind is achieved, it is likely that the High Priestess relays Otherworld messages.

This work includes "Charges' relating to each Moon phase with the corresponding aspect of the
Goddess, consistent with the Cycle of Birth, Life, Death and Rebirth as manifest in Nature around us.

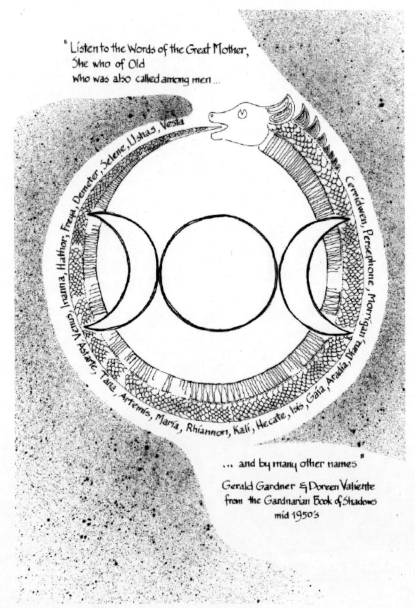

" Listen to the Words of the Great Mother,
She who of Old
Who was also called among men ...

... and by many other names "

Gerald Gardner & Doreen Valiente
from the Gardnarian Book of Shadows
mid 1950's

Drawing Down the Moon

Just before The Charge is said, the HPS stands with her back to the Altar in the
Osiris pose with the Wand in the right hand and the Athame in the left, her
wrists are crossed as are the tools.
The HP kneels before her, arms outstretched with palms facing towards the HPS

He says:

I honour the Goddess who resides within you
Love and power your body to imbue
I bless thy skin
Goddess kin
I bless each bone
Goddess throne
I bless thy veins
Goddess higher planes
I bless thy mind
Goddess thoughts kind
I bless thy eyes
Goddess skies
I bless thy voice
Goddess message we rejoice
I bless thy heart
Of the Goddess ye are part
I bless thy seeing
Goddess being
I bless thy seed
Goddess creed
Ye, our Goddess One
Universe, Moon and Sun

The HPS moves into Isis pose, arms outstretched, feet apart ,still holding Ritual
tools
HP is still kneeling in front of her.
HP says:

I call on You Great Goddess to cast aside this Veil
Transcend time and space and scale
Great Mother, source of Life Force
Great Mother, Spring of Energy Source
Origin of the One and the All
Please harken to my call
For by seed and root
From bud to shoot
From flower to fruit
I invoke You to imbue this body whole
It's mind and soul
This priestess, Yours
This day and more scores
Bless us with Your presence, power
At this sacred Esbat hour

All Coveners, except the HP and HPS stand and sing in soft repeat refrain with
soft fade out:

We honour You
To always see us through
We honour You
Blessings to ensue

HP is still kneeling holding his arms outwards and forwards with palms facing
the HPS.
HP says:

Beautiful and proud
Gone is the gossamer shroud
Behold Aradia, pure and gentle
Shining light and Spirit Elemental
Crossed the Threshold
As we behold

The true Divine
In love and Joyful shine
As we stand in awe
Behold, Aradia - the Goddess we adore
Is nigh, under this indigo sky
She shows Her sign
Merciful, benign
Fire, water, smoke and chalice wine
Desire, mystery cloak unveiled so fine

HP stands back as the HPS draws the Invoking Pentagram of the Earth in front of him

HPS says:

Great Mother of the Origin Source
Guide to all Life's course
The womb, the grail, the spark, the whole
The great Divinity within our Soul

The HPS replaces her tools on the Altar. The HP and HPS stand side by side and face the Coven standing to the south and west of the Altar

HP speaks the introductory words by
Doreen Valiente and Gerald Gardner from the Gardnarian Book of Shadows

"Listen to the Words of the Great Mother
She who of old was also called among men Artemis,
Astarte, Athene, Dione, Melusine,
Aphrodite, Cerridwen, Dana, Arianrhod, Isis,
Bride and by many other names"

Note: The original words of The Charge were written by
Gerald Gardner as found in a document dating from 1949.
His words are based on those written and researched by
Charles Godfrey Leland in his book:
Aradia or the Gospel of the Witches,
Phoenix Publishing, Inc. USA. 1998. ISBN 0-919345-34-4

The Charge is based on the words which Aradia speaks to her daughter, Diana and her followers.

Waxing Moon- Maiden- Mother

- First stirrings of Promise
- New Beginnings and Growing Manifestation
- Evolution and Unfolding Clarity of Consciousness
- Increasing Energy and Psychic vibration

Dark Moon- The Enchantress

Full Moon-
The Great Mother

Waning Moon-Crone

- Initiation of Change and Banishment
- Introspection, Reflection and Consolidation
- Ebbing Energy Flow and Slowing Psychic Vibration
- Application of Wisdom, Inception of Concepts

The Charge of the Goddess

First Quarter - Waxing Moon

Maiden Mother Charge

Open your eyes and see the Beginning
The origins of all Life brimming
For I am the Source
The Origin and the Force
I am the womb of your birth
The Creator of the Earth
I am the maker of the Universe
The Planes of Spiritual disperse
I am the energy pre-existent
Of time long distant
I am the divine indwelling
Your spirit insight welling

I am your Guide on your Quest
And will hearken at your behest
For I can lead you to the One and the All
If you hearken to my call
I am yours to revere
If you care to hear
For truth and learning I bestow
To all who wish to know
I can wisdom inspire
For all who enquire
For I am that voice in the night
That hears your lonely plight

So, do not ignore me!
But, turn to adore me
For here is the hand that I proffer
As the true Self I offer
So step up with courage and boldness
Leave behind the ignorant coldness
And uncover your strength latent
To shine in confidence patent

For I am within you
By many given clue
As you are within me
Look inside to see!

I am the source of your wishes and dreams
The cause of stirring emotion streams
I am that fleeting thought
By the unconscious wrought
I am your deepest yearning
For understanding learning

So take my hand and walk that journey
Of Life, from birth to Requiem gurney
As by the Silver Bough you depart the here and now
For I know the All and have transcended the pall
For within me you shall find peace
To all questions that never cease

The trees and mountains by my hands made
Like the seed to bud to shoot to leafy blade
The grand celestial station is my creation
For I am pre-existent Elemental
And wholly transcendental

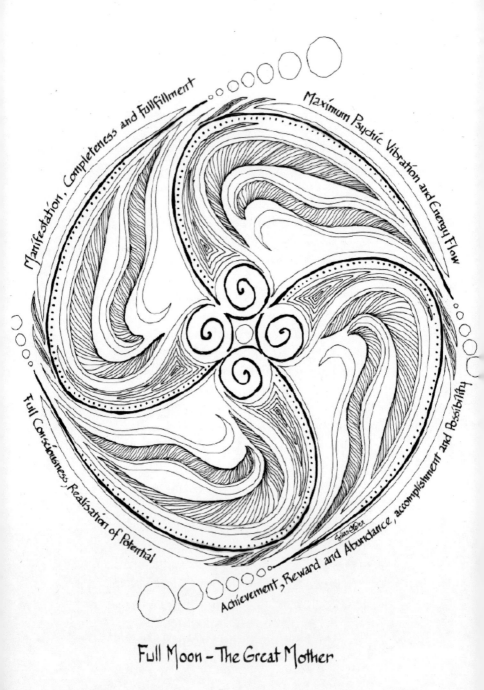

Manifestation, Completeness and Fullfillment

Maximum Psychic Vibration and Energy Flow

Full Consciousness, Realization of Potential

Achievement, Reward and Abundance, accomplishment and Possibility

Full Moon - The Great Mother

The Charge of the Goddess
Second Quarter - Full Moon

Great Mother Charge

Concept inspired by 'The Charge' as written by
Doreen Valiente and Gerald Gardner

Rewritten by Silver Elder

HPS says:
When ever ye should feel the need
To be from deprivation freed
Feel free to ask
No matter how small the task
For I am there for you
Honest reliable and true
We shall gather at our special venue
And regard our mutual menu
At our unique Esbat meeting place
I shall transcend time and space
To be with ye all
And heed your call

Time and space shall I transcend
For time with ye to spend

I shall know your true intent
And depth, consideration spent
And grant all wishes pure
Those honest, true and sure

As the God and Goddess, One and All
I stride the divide and cast aside the Pall
And see through every screen
And witness every scene

It is my true delight
On each Esbat - Sabbat night
To extend my reach
For wisdom to teach
For empathy and Magick
To heal the sad and tragic
To show the Craft of spell casting
For all needs to Handfasting
To impart the science of bi-location
And astral travel, transmutation
For I am the wisdom source
The all-knowledgeable power force
Also the Maiden, Mother, Crone
For all divine skills to hone

I wish to teach all who hear
Open mind and keen in ear
I tell them this
To achieve your bliss
Strive for the highest ideal
Yours to sign and seal
Ensure a heart that's pure
And intent that's honourable, sure
And never to waver
For temptation to savor
For this is your test
To achieve your highest quest
As you responsibility show
And right from wrong you know

Abide by the Wiccan Rede
To be equal in race, color, creed
For you, I will cross the divide
To be by your side
Across space and time
To achieve your goals sublime

I am the Queen of Life, incarnate
To all, whether poor or those in State
I govern life's transition from birth
Into the Otherworld realms from Earth
A life of bliss and peace
From birth, decease
Once past the test of Karmic Law
You're ready to enter the Otherworld Door
As there to further learn
For all wisdom that you yearn
For all I will impart
From my deepest, kindest heart

Through me your true self'l shine
With a heart so pure divine
Through me your soul'l unfold
Through wisdom pure unscrolled
Through me expanded is your mind
With thought intent so kind
For I am the All Cosmic Queen
Felt and sensed unseen
I am your wish granted
All seed fertile planted
I am the divine and universal force
The infinite cosmic power source
For within me, in my love thou shalt reside
As over your life's path I shall preside
I am the everlasting Will

The divine unfailing skill

As I have been with you from the start
For we shall never part

But of you I do ask this
In order to enter the realms of Bliss
You need to know the Mystery
If you wish to seek and find me
If you cant find me within
Deep in your heart, under your skin
You shall not find me without
Outside and round about
For the powers in you do reside
In heart, mind, spirit, deep inside
For I am the All and All is in me
For I am One with the Universe
- And also in ye!

I am the Universal Cosmic Fire
The One who fulfils your hearts desire
I will you in all life to rejoice
And to hear my loving voice
As I bid you to partake
And this solemn Vow to make
That you shall the highest standard uphold
And work for what's right, strong and bold
For love and virtue are my Ritual
And my ideals habitual
And this is in thee, what I seek
And this is why I call and speak
To plane the path and smooth the way
To do what's good, without delay

I am the Ruler of Nature's Wheel

The Queen of Divine will and seal
Once you have found your inner divine spark
And feel you strong enough to make the mark
I shall respond to the wave of your wand
And be your constant friend
Till your life's end
To once return
For you to live and learn
Across the Otherworld divide
To be once again, by your side

I am the Great Goddess Four Fold
In four aspects to behold
Maiden, Mother, Enchantress and Crone
Encompassing all of life's wisdoms known
I am the Ruler of the Moon phase
My symbol, in grand silvery blaze
In life's pulse, new life shall ensue
As I evolve, waxing, waning, full and new
And as by my pure and silver light
You gather for your Monthly Esbat Rite
You shall not take fright
But practice in your psychic might
At Full Moons peek and height
As I shall appear in life, love and joy
As real incarnate, your cosmic envoy
As by the sweep of your wand, I shall respond
As by the direction of thine athame
I shall appear and you shall see
As with my angels, Elementals all assembled here
And kindred spirits from far and near
We shall celebrate in joy and peace
For healing powers to release

All channeling and Otherworld messages happen here

As part of the grounding done after any energy work,
the Coven sings softly in repeat Choral:

UNDER MOON AND SACRED STAR

Under Moon and Sacred Star
Calling Energies from near and far
Let us celebrate and sing
Rejoice in our special gathering
All evil to banish
Hatred to vanish
To darkness bring light
Energy bright
To celebrate our Lady and Lord
By Athame, Wand and Sword
For we honour Thee
So mote it be!

Repeat refrain:
For we honour Thee
So mote it be!

For we honour Thee
So mote it be!

For we honour Thee
So mote it be!

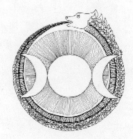

Waxing Moon - Maiden - Mother

◎ First stirrings of Promise
◎ New Beginnings and Growing Manifestation
◎ Evolution and Unfolding Clarity of Consciousness
◎ Increasing Energy and Psychic vibration

Dark Moon - The Enchantress

Full Moon - The Great Mother

Waning Moon - Crone

◎ Initiation of Change and Banishment
◎ Introspection, Reflection and Consolidation
◎ Ebbing Energy Flow and Slowing Psychic Vibration
◎ Application of Wisdom, Inception of Concepts

The Charge of the Goddess
Third Quarter - Waning Moon

The Crone Charge

Welcome to my Temple of Old
I am awaiting you, scared but bold
Like you, I walked the path and found the hearth
And I am the light blaze at the core of the maze
My door stands open and invites
All who seek the Mysteries' insights
And those who did succumb
Were freed from dark and dumb
To be reborn anew
In visionary quest and clue
From their thrashing ignorance released
Their Ego long deceased
For I am the Crone and the Wise
Who leads you to the Enchantress' surprise

I promise life eternal
By the Souls' renewal journal
As my embrace signals the end of the Ego chase
To welcome the decision
The key of life's transition
The true knowledge quest
And ultimate test
Of finding the Self in a mind expanded

By joint polarity landed

Such is my Change
That expands the psychic range
For I am the forked road Trivia
That sends darkness to Oblivia
As I hold the key to personal growth
And hold you to your private oath

So, look me in the face
And step to my embrace
As the Ruler of the Moon
I impart the wisdom boon
I am the keeper of the Propylaea Gate
Step inside!, for insight running spate
I am the sign-post
To the true knowledge host

I am the bearer of the light
In your deepest darkest night
I hold the key
To your confounding mystery
I have the power to reveal
And the Grail unseal!

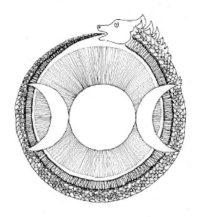

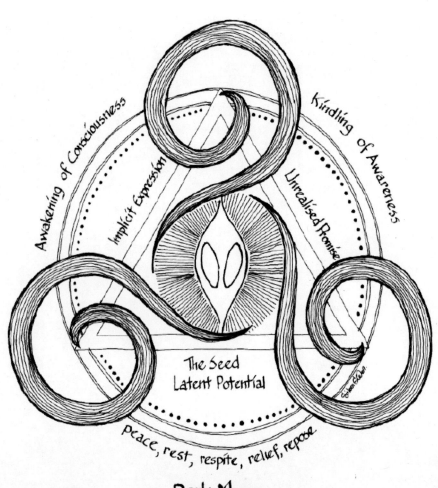

Awakening of Consciousness

Kindling of Awareness

Implicit Expression

Unrealised Promise

The Seed
Latent Potential

peace, rest, respite, relief, repose

Dark Moon
The Enchantress

The Charge of the Goddess

Fourth Quarter - Dark Moon

Enchantress

I am the Goddess Triple Mother
All powerful like non other
I am known by many names
And given many claims
But I am the One and the All
And I am within you through the Seasons to the Fall
I am the maiden, Mother, Crone
The Moon, the Earth, the Universe, my throne
I am the One in Three
And I dwell within thee!
I am the changing Moon from Dark to Full
With energies waning, waxing, pull
I am the Cycle season
The warmth and coldness reason
Autumn, Winter, Spring
Its new hope that I bring
And the Summer harvest time
That bumper crop sublime

I am the draining power, the growing cold
I am the waning hour and the growing old
But I am the promise of rebirth
Within the higher realms of my creation, Earth
For I am life eternal and infinite
The Circle with no end in sight

Over your incarnations, I preside
Once you pass the Requiem Divide
I am the insight wisdom sought
The Ego transformation wrought
I am the latent feminine in men
Their other half in ken
It's the light spark to the Dark Lord I bring
As Natures song I sing
As the Grail is my womb
The wellspring of creation
From birth, to life, to tomb
Throughout the celestial station
For I am the beginning primordial
And older than time immemorial

I am the sunrise due East
At your Ostara – Mabon feast
I am the mother of Yule's Sun Child
The hope of rebirth mild
I am the bearer of the Light at your Imbolc Rite
The liberator from the cold for latent life unfold
At Ostara from the Underworld I return
As the ever stronger life force yearns
At Beltane, free in love am I
As I sense our God, the Green Man nigh
For on this night we mate
As Sun and Earth for growth in spate
At Litha, I share the throne
With my Sun King consort adult grown
But by the harvest scythe he's assailed
As by Lughnasadh his powers failed
At Mabon I search and find
My consort Dark Lord kind
And by the Western Portal I choose to leave
The Earth turns cold and begins to grieve

At Samhain as the Souls roam free
I ignite the spark for my Lord to see
That I am in him and he is in me
For we are the same, the pair in binary
I am the endless cycle of Nature infinite
The birth, the life, the death, the darkness light
I am the sun rise, midday and Sun's demise

I am the Goddess of many faces
Worshipped in countless places
I am the new day dawn, the germinating corn
I am the western Sun's demise
And the eastern silver Moon's rise
I am the infinite cycles turn
The glow of the Moon and the Sun's warm burn
I am the waning, waxing, ebbing flow
The decline and quickening grow
I am the equidistant light and dark
At the Eastern-Western Quarter midway mark
I am always the light in the dark
The latent fire in the spark
I am the promise of change
Throughout the infinite range
I am motion perpetual
The endless cycle conceptual
I am existence without end
The infinite I transcend

For such is my aspect trine
Transcendent, true, divine.

Recommended Reading List

Adler, Margot
    Drawing Down the Moon; Witches, Druids,
    Goddess Worshippers and other Pagans in America
    today
    Penguin Compass/ Penguin Group USA. 1986.

Bonewits, Isaac.,
    Bonewits's Essential Guide to Druidism
    Citadel Press, Kensington Publishing Corp. USA.
    2006

Buckland, Raymond.,
    Buckland's Complete Book of Witchcraft, Second
    and Revised Edition
    Llewellyn Publications, USA. 2004

Campbell, Joseph with Bill Moyers
    The Power of Myth
    Doubleday, a division of Bantam Doubleday Dell
    Publishing Group, Inc. USA. 1988

    The Mythic Image
    Bollingen Series C, Princeton University Press,
    USA. 1974

Carr-Gomm, Philip.,
    Druidcraft, the Magic of Wicca and Druidry
    Thorsons, an imprint of HarperCollins Publishers,
    UK. 2002

    Druid Mysteries, Ancient Wisdom for the 21st
    Century
    Rider, an imprint of Ebury Press, UK. 2002

In the Grove of the Druids, the Druid Teachings of
Ross Nichols
Watkins Publishing, UK. 2002

Conway, D.J.,
Wicca, The Complete Craft
The Crossing Press, USA. 2001

Crowley, Vivianne, PhD.
Wicca, A Comprehensive Guide to the Old Religion
in the Modern World
Element, Harper Collins Publishers, UK, 2003

Cunningham, Scott.,
Wicca, a Guide for the Solitary Practitioner
Llewellyn Publications, USA. 2005

de Angeles, Ly.,
Witchcraft, Theory and Practice
Llewellyn Publications, USA, 2004

Eliade, Mircea, Prof.
Images and Symbols, Studies in Religious
Symbolism
Mythos, an imprint of the Princeton University
Press, USA. 1991

Shamanism, Archaic Techniques of Ecstasy
Arkana, published by the Penguin Group, UK. 1989

Occultism, Witchcraft and Cultural Fashions,
Essays in Comparative Religions.
University of Chicago Press, USA. 1976

Farrar, Janet and Stewart.,
A Witches' Bible, the Complete Witches' Handbook
Phoenix Publishing, Inc. USA. 1984

Farrar, Janet and Stewart with Gavin Bone
The Healing Craft, Healing Practices for Witches
and Pagans
Phoenix Publishing, Inc. USA. 1999

Gimbutas, Marija, Prof.
The Living Goddess, edited and supplemented by
Miriam Robbins Dexter, PhD.
University of California Press, USA. 2001

González-Wippler, Migene.,
Book of Shadows
Llewellyn Publications, USA. 2005

The Complete Book of Spells, Ceremonies and
Magic
Llewellyn Publications, USA. 2004

Grimassi, Raven.,
The Wiccan Mysteries, Ancient Origins and
Teachings
Llewellyn Publications, USA. 2004

Witchcraft, a Mystery Tradition
Llewellyn Publications, USA. 2004

The Witches' Craft, The Roots of Witchcraft and
Magical Transformation
Llewellyn Publications, USA. 2002

Hillman, James.

Re-visioning Psychology
HarperPerenial, a division of HarperCollins
Publishers, USA. 1992

Hutton, Ronald, Prof. PhD.,
    The Triumph of the Moon, a History of Modern
    Pagan Witchcraft
    Oxford University Press Inc. UK. 1999

Jung, Carl Gustav Prof. PhD. M.-L. von Franz PhD.,
Joseph L. Henderson, PhD., Jolande Jacobi, PhD., Aniela
Jaffe,
    Man and his Symbols
    Picador, an imprint of Pan Macmillan Ltd. UK. 1964

Jung, Carl Gustav Prof. PhD.
    Modern Man in Search of Soul, Translated by
    W.S.Dell
    Routledge and Kegan Paul Ltd. UK. 1978

    Psychology and Alchemy, Translated by R.F.C.
    Hull
    Routledge, UK, reprinted 1989

    Psychology and the Occult, Translated by R.F.C.
    Hull
    Bollingen Series XX, Princeton University Press,
    USA. 1990

    Synchronicity, An Acausal Connecting Principle
    Routledge, an imprint of Taylor and Francis Group,
    UK. 2006

Leland, Charles G.
    Aradia of the Gospel of the Witches, a new

Translation by Mario Pazzaglini, PhD. and Dina
Pazzaglini
Phoenix Publishing Inc. USA. 1998

Matthews, Caitlín and John,
Walkers between the Worlds, the Western
Mysteries from Shaman to Magus
Inner Traditions International, USA. 2004

McCoy, Edain.,
Advanced Witchcraft, Go Deeper, Reach Further,
Fly Higher
Llewellyn Publications, USA. 2004

Moura, Ann.,
Green Magic, The Sacred Connection to Nature
Llewellyn Publications, USA. 2003

Neuman, Erich, PhD.
The Great Mother, an Analysis of the Archetype,
Translated by Ralph Manheim
Mythos, Bollingen Series XLVII, Princeton
University Press, 1974

Raven Wolf, Silver.,
To Ride a Silver Broomstick, New Generation
Witchcraft
Llewellyn Publications, USA. 2005

To Stir a Magick Cauldron, a Witches' Guide to
Conjuring and Casting
Llewellyn Publications, USA. 2003

Restall Orr, Emma.,
Living Druidry, Magical Spirituality for the Wild

Soul
Piatkus Books Ltd. UK, 2004

Starhawk
The Spiral Dance, a Rebirth of the Ancient Religion
of the Great Goddess
Harper SanFrancisco/ HarperCollins Publishers Inc.
USA. 1999

Talboys, Greame K.,
The Way of the Druid, The Renaissance of a Celtic
Religion and its Relevance for Today
O-Books, an Imprint of The Bothy, John Hunt
Publishing Ltd. UK. 2005

Valiente, Doreen.,
Natural Magic
Phoenix Publishing Inc. USA, 1975

Witchcraft for Tomorrow
Phoenix Publishing Inc. USA. 1978

BOOKS

O is a symbol of the world, of oneness and unity. In different
cultures it also means the "eye," symbolizing knowledge and
insight. We aim to publish books that are accessible, constructive
and that challenge accepted opinion, both that of academia and
the "moral majority."

Our books are available in all good English language
bookstores worldwide. If you don't see the book on the shelves
ask the bookstore to order it for you, quoting the ISBN number
and title. Alternatively you can order online (all major online
retail sites carry our titles) or contact the distributor in the
relevant country, listed on the copyright page.

See our website **www.o-books.net** for a full list of over 500
titles, growing by 100 a year.

And tune in to myspiritradio.com for our book review radio show,
hosted by June-Elleni Laine, where you can listen to the authors
discussing their books.

MySpiritRadio